American Patriots

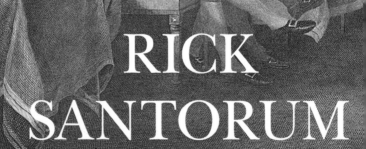

AMERICAN PATRIOTS

Answering the Call to Freedom

★ ★ ★

RICK SANTORUM

Visit Tyndale online at www.tyndale.com.

TYNDALE and Tyndale's quill logo are registered trademarks of Tyndale House Publishers, Inc.

American Patriots: Answering the Call to Freedom

Designed by Erik M. Peterson

Published in association with Ambassador Literary Agency, Nashville, TN.

Unless otherwise indicated, all Scripture quotations are taken from the *Holy Bible*, King James Version.

Scripture quotations marked NLT are taken from the *Holy Bible*, New Living Translation, copyright © 1996, 2004, 2007 by Tyndale House Foundation. Used by permission of Tyndale House Publishers, Inc., Carol Stream, Illinois 60188. All rights reserved.

Scripture quotations marked NIV are taken from the Holy Bible, *New International Version,*® NIV.® Copyright © 1973, 1978, 1984, 2011 by Biblica, Inc.™ Used by permission of Zondervan. All rights reserved worldwide. www.zondervan.com.

Scripture quotations marked NKJV are taken from the New King James Version.® Copyright © 1982 by Thomas Nelson, Inc. Used by permission. All rights reserved.

Scripture quotations marked ESV are taken from *The Holy Bible*, English Standard Version® (ESV®), copyright © 2001 by Crossway, a publishing ministry of Good News Publishers. Used by permission. All rights reserved.

Scripture texts marked NAB are taken from the *New American Bible*, revised edition © 2010, 1991, 1986, 1970 Confraternity of Christian Doctrine, Washington, DC, and are used by permission of the copyright owner. All rights reserved. No part of the *New American Bible* may be reproduced in any form without permission in writing from the copyright owner.

Library of Congress Cataloging-in-Publication Data

Santorum, Rick, date.
  American patriots : answering the call to freedom / Rick Santorum.
    p. cm.
  Includes bibliographical references.
  ISBN 978-1-4143-7908-1 (hc)
1. United States—History—Revolution, 1775-1783—Biography. 2. United States—History—Revolution, 1775-1783—Religious aspects. 3. United States—Church history—18th century. 4. Christianity and politics—United States—History—18th century. 5. Church and state—United States—History—18th century. I. Title.
E209.S27 2012
973.3—dc23   2012027808

Printed in the United States of America

18	17	16	15	14	13	12
8	7	6	5	4	3	2

To all our forgotten heroes, past and present,

in and out of uniform, who have sacrificed much—

and at times all—so we might be free.

Contents

Foreword

In the course of human history, the story of America's founding is high and unique. There are few narratives quite as romantic or quite as profound as the unlikely birth of this nation.

Together, farmers, traders, statesmen, and colonists of all stripes altered the course of history and ushered in a constitutional republic—the first of its kind. We, the beneficiaries of such a republic, cannot forget their story, for it is our story as well. It was born of reflection, baptized with blood, and has become the morning and evening star of freedom, the standard by which other nations are judged and judge themselves.

It is the story of Patriots, both known and unknown—people like John Laurens, Nancy Morgan Hart, Lydia Darragh, and Haym Salomon. Do these names mean anything to you? They should. These men and women were not generals or presidents, but they were heroes of the Revolution nonetheless. Without them, the account of America's founding would be dramatically different.

American Patriots: Answering the Call to Freedom tells

their stories, along with those of other equally important Patriots. Their stories will surprise you, delight you, and remind you of the difference individual men and women can make in the pursuit of life, liberty, and happiness. Leaders shape nations, but not without the work of many calloused hands, such as the ones described in this book. These early-American Patriots will inspire you to preserve what they so nobly fought for.

The timing of this book couldn't be more critical. Right now our country is engaged in serious national debate over the future course of this nation—a path toward autonomous, individual responsibility or a path toward an overreaching, intrusive caretaker. Our fate is not certain. Too many citizens today do not know these early American Patriots or understand why they fought and what they fought for. Sadly, US history is the worst subject for our high school seniors.

The burden falls on each of us to raise and educate a generation that understands its precious founding. William Wordsworth wrote, "What we have loved / Others will love, and we will teach them how." Without an active, informed citizenry, we risk becoming alien to the nation we inhabit.

Perhaps no cultural or political leader today grasps this better than Rick Santorum. It is entirely fitting that the son of hardworking Catholic Italian immigrants be the one to tell the story of America's great, but often overlooked, Patriots. From his time in the US Senate to his candidacy for presidential nominee, Santorum has defended the defenseless and spoken on behalf of those with voices often drowned out by popular culture or secular media.

In this important, timely book, Santorum stands up for some of our forgotten American Patriots, reminding us through historical narratives and compelling profiles of the unlikely voices that answered the call to defend freedom. This book, above all, should inspire a new generation of American patriots to rise up and defend the cause of liberty. The fate of the republic was at stake then, and the same may be true today.

William J. Bennett

Acknowledgments

Most Americans know something about our Founding Fathers and their role in creating the government of the United States. However, most know little about the day-to-day battles fought by Americans of all backgrounds that paved the way for the high ideals of our founders to be put into practice. In many cases, it was indeed the "little guys" who stepped up in big ways to forge our liberty.

Telling the stories of these founders is an honor but also a challenge. There are so many Revolutionary heroes and heroines from all walks of life. In reviewing the sources, I was amazed that so many were just regular folk raised up by God for such a time as this. I have no doubt that these people who were involved in the Revolution suspected they were participating in a consequential time in the course of human history.

However, the resource material, particularly with respect to frontline soldiers and common civilians, often comes from second- or thirdhand recollections. So the job of culling potential candidates from long lists for this book, separating fact from fiction, and uncovering the necessary details that animate the individuals profiled was no easy undertaking. That task was ably performed by our research team, led by Michael Leaser and assisted by Benjamin Kafferlin. They did the hard work of providing me the best-documented material to first decide whom to include in the book and then to faithfully relate their stories. Thank you both for your excellent, thorough, and promptly submitted work. Well done.

As with my first book, I wouldn't have done this project without the encouragement, insight, and support of Mark Rodgers. In one capacity or another, we have been working together in and out of public life for twenty-two incredibly productive years. I am grateful to Mark for being a great navigator for the cause over the years.

Writing a book is never easy on family life. While my son Daniel added a few beautiful lines to this book, the other children helped in the best way they could—they encouraged me to take the time to work on the manuscript and picked up the slack around the house to make it all work. Karen and I are very blessed to have such thoughtful and generous children.

Like any endeavor in my life, this one would have been impossible without the support and assistance of my wife, Karen. Doing what she does every day in my life is support enough. As a mother of seven, including our special little girl, Bella, she already has her plate full, but she still found time to review and edit throughout this process. It is a much better book as a result.

Introduction

I've always felt blessed to have grown up in a home with an immigrant parent whose father brought him to this country in search of freedom and opportunity. As a child, I knew that the people I loved and respected the most had chosen to be Americans. I was told repeatedly that this country wasn't just a better place than their homeland; it was the best country in the world.

My grandfather came to America in 1923 from the region of northern Italy that had been part of Austria until after World War I. Unlike most Italian immigrants of that time, he didn't come because of economic hardship—he had a good job working on a mail train. He came because after fighting for a warmongering, erratic leader and being severely wounded on the Russian front, he saw in Benito Mussolini another tyrant in the making. There were other countries in Europe he could have immigrated to where he would have been closer to his eight brothers and sisters, but he chose America. The United States was not just the land of economic opportunity; it was also where people went to be free from such tyrants.

Like millions of other immigrants, my grandfather became an American the moment he walked through the gates of Ellis Island. Had he decided to move to France or Germany, he could have lived there for forty years and still not been considered French or German. From its beginning, the United States has been different from every other country in the history of the world. America is not about birthrights, classes, or bloodlines. We are not a tribe or an ethnic group or a civilization with a long written history on this continent.

America is an ideal—a set of common values that unite us not only as states, but as a people. Those ideals were expressed at the very founding of our country in the Declaration of Independence and reinforced in the United States Constitution.

We rightly revere these documents, but we also need to honor the Patriots who wrote them and the men and women who fought and sacrificed not just to win independence but also to set inspiring examples that would bring these documents—and indeed, our country—to life.

In the history of our nation, it has always been the individuals who embraced the ideals laid out by our founders who have made America such a great country. And so it is today, with a rebirth of citizen groups stressing the importance of our founding documents as still-relevant guides for governing the United States.

In recent decades, the idea that the Constitution is a "living, breathing document" has created a legal playground for liberals to attempt to transform society. But now conservatives have reinjected into the main discourse of politics the Constitution's limits on federal governmental power. This concept is being asserted to preserve America's founding principles.

The Constitution is a vital document. It is the *how* of America—the operator's manual for our government. But as we see from years of judicial activism, the Constitution can be massaged to chart a course very different from the one our founders intended.

Unless the Constitution is anchored to something that gives it context and meaning, it could become a dangerous document, like the early constitutions of revolutionary France in the 1790s. Inspired in many ways by the American Revolution and our new Constitution, the French seemed to be heading down the same path as America with the passage of a similar constitution establishing a French Republic.

Yet the French Revolution, based on the seemingly high-minded concepts of liberty, equality, and fraternity, resulted in a republic marked by a reign of terror that collapsed within a decade.

America succeeded and has endured because both the Revolution and our operator's manual, the Constitution, were anchored to a different foundation in an all-important way. That anchor—the *why* of America, the heart of who we are as a nation—can be found in the words of the Declaration of Independence:

We hold these truths to be self-evident, that all men are created equal, that they are endowed by their Creator with certain unalienable Rights, that among these are Life, Liberty and the pursuit of Happiness.

Like revolutionary France, our founders rooted this document in the concepts of equality and liberty. But unlike French leaders, our Founding Fathers recognized that our rights come not from *fraternity* (that is, from each other or, more accurately, from the government) but from *paternity* (the God of Abraham, Isaac, and Jacob). The acknowledgment that our rights come from God, not the government, separates the United States from every other country in the world.

The Constitution has succeeded as a framework for our republic because the government it establishes is inherently limited, not being the source of human rights. Further, the founders put strict limits on federal power. Our founders believed in limited government and the unlimited God-given potential of the American people.

The concepts I have described were at one time truly revolutionary ideas advanced by a relatively small group of freedom fighters who changed the course of human history. These Patriots were not just rebelling against the king of England; they were standing up to thousands of years of the elites ruling the masses. Undaunted, these brave individuals concluded the Declaration of Independence with the following oath:

With a firm reliance on the protection of divine Providence, we mutually pledge to each other our Lives, our Fortunes and our sacred Honor.

The founders who affixed their names to this radical document, as well as the other Patriots who upheld it in word and deed, truly did risk all. Patrick Henry's famous exhortation to the Virginia colonial legislature in 1775, "Give me liberty, or give me death," was the choice made by every Patriot featured in this book. Every revolutionary, from baker and pastor to ship captain and soldier, was committing treason against the British Crown and faced lengthy imprisonment or execution if captured.

While the Patriots described on these pages may not be household names today, most of them were well known at the time of the Revolution. They were people from every walk of life who rose to meet the challenge of their day and, in so doing, set forth a template that would inspire future generations of citizen patriots.

While the American Patriots of the Revolution accomplished the monumental task of establishing freedom, it has been the responsibility of every subsequent generation to maintain that freedom. As Ronald Reagan said, "Freedom is a fragile thing and is never more than one generation away from extinction. It is not ours by inheritance; it must be fought for and defended constantly by each generation, for it comes only once to a people. Those who have known freedom and then lost it have never known it again." He was right, and like the Patriots brought to life in these pages, we are now the ones responsible for upholding that legacy.

Today we are facing a threat to the very foundation our founders laid. That threat does not come from an alien force but from those who are willing and determined to abandon the concept of God-given rights. Like the royalty during the Revolution, today's elites wish to return to the pre-Revolutionary paradigm in which they, through governmental force, allocate rights and responsibilities.

George Washington warned us of this danger: "Government is not reason, it is not eloquence—it is force! Like fire, it is a dangerous servant and a fearful master. Never for a moment should it be left to irresponsible action."

My hope is that these stories inspire you, as they did me, to put on the cap of citizenship and fight for freedom. It is our watch. Like every generation of Americans, we are called to be good stewards of this great inheritance. After reading these stories, I hope you, like these Patriots, feel blessed to be living at a time when our country, which is the hope of the world, needs you.

Rick Santorum

Part I

★ ★ ★

LIFE

L ife, Liberty and the pursuit of Happiness." Couldn't Jefferson just as easily have written these enumerated rights, given to all by our Creator, in a different order? Liberty, happiness, and life? Or happiness, life, and liberty? The answer, of course, is that he could have written them in any order. But he made this decision consciously, knowing that each right is foundational for the next.

Is it possible to have liberty if you are denied the right to life? Can you pursue happiness if you are not free to do so? The founders logically ordered the rights to build on each other—from foundational to aspirational.

Life is clearly the foundational right. Our founders saw the government's first and highest priority as the protection of life. It was obvious to them that all other rights were meaningless if life was denied or diminished. It is hard to fathom that any principle could have a broader consensus in our country than the belief that every American has the right to live.

However, American history is stained with examples of people who were denied this basic right. So perhaps it is not so surprising that of our country's basic rights, the right to life is at the core of the most contentious struggle.

The Declaration also states that all men are created equal. From the beginning, our founders set forth this revolutionary principle that runs counter to most cultures: all human life is of equal value and should be treated equally under the law. Although this ideal did not become a reality for all groups of people at the time, it is undeniable that this core belief set the foundation for equal treatment in our country.

What is the origin of this radical concept that all are created equal? It certainly doesn't come from scientific observation, since no two people are identical, physically or mentally. We should be treated equally for one compelling reason: because we are equal in the eyes of the Creator—the God of Abraham, Isaac, and Jacob.

Until the Revolution, the concept of all men being created equal flew in the face of thousands of years of human history. Man has drawn distinctions among people based on various criteria—race, creed, gender, age, or ethnicity. These discriminations, of course, have resulted in the most horrific of human tragedies. Man's inhumanity to man has been present in every civilization, and despite the greatness of American society, our government—usually with the support of a vocal and powerful minority—has been guilty of denying equal treatment to all humans.

While we, like our founders, struggle to live and govern in concert with the truths of the Declaration, there is no ambiguity or uncertainty in the document. The founders said that *all* of us are endowed by our Creator with the right to life. An endowment is not something that is merited; it is a gift. Of course, life itself is a mysterious gift from God, but the right to life is not something to be earned or created. Your God-given right to life, as recognized in the Declaration, is attached to you the moment your life starts. The government has been entrusted with respecting and protecting that right.

Although the idea of all life being sacred was not put into practice in most pre-Revolutionary societies, this concept is deeply rooted in Western civilization. It is clear that according to earliest Judeo-Christian thought, life is considered to begin at conception:

For you created my inmost being;
  you knit me together in my mother's womb.
I praise you because I am fearfully and wonderfully made;
  your works are wonderful,
  I know that full well.
My frame was not hidden from you
  when I was made in the secret place,
  when I was woven together in the depths of the earth.
Your eyes saw my unformed body;
  all the days ordained for me were written in your book
  before one of them came to be.

PSALM 139:13-16, NIV

Not surprisingly, this biblical understanding found its way into British common law, which to a large degree is the basis for the US legal code. William Blackstone, an eighteenth-century British judge and jurist, was a favorite authority of our founders. Blackstone's commentaries—widely considered the definitive work on British common law—are still a required reference in many law schools today.

Judge Blackstone laid out quite clearly when life is to be protected:

> Life is the immediate gift of God, a right
> inherent by nature in every individual: and it
> begins in contemplation of law as soon as an
> infant is able to stir in the mother's womb.
> For if a woman is quick with child, and by a
> potion or otherwise, kill[s] it in her womb; or
> if any one beat her, whereby the child die[s] in
> her body, and she is delivered of a dead child;
> this . . . was by the ancient law homicide or
> manslaughter.

With the aid of technology, we now know that life doesn't begin when a mother feels the child stir in the womb but at the moment of conception—the union between the sperm and the ovum. At that moment, a new human being is created with unique DNA. The zygote is biologically human and metabolizing and therefore alive. By definition, this constitutes a human life.

Today our country is deeply divided over this most basic right to human life, and that controversy is not limited to life in the womb. The same issues are at stake for the sick, the elderly, and those with disabilities. My wife, Karen, and I have personally faced this struggle on behalf of our daughter Bella, who was born with a condition that limits both her physical and her mental development. Many ethicists and physicians recommend abortion or denial of care after birth for individuals with such diagnoses, and we have had to fight at times to receive appropriate medical care for her.

Ultimately our culture is not so different from

Revolutionary America. We, too, must struggle to ensure that the right to life is granted to everyone—including those who don't have a voice to speak for themselves.

As the stories in this book highlight, the foundational right to life has always been the core moral issue of our country. These Patriots were willing to see beyond the situational ethics of their day and their own financial interests to courageously fight for truth and the dignity of *all* human life.

PETER FRANCISCO

The Virginia Giant

★ ★ ★

*The Spirit of the LORD came powerfully upon him. . . . Finding a fresh
jawbone of a donkey, he grabbed it and struck down a thousand men.*

JUDGES 15:14-15, NIV

At the heart of the fundamental right to life
is a belief that every life is a gift and will
make a contribution to society if given the
chance. Or, as I was taught as a child, God doesn't
make mistakes. There is no better example of this
principle during the Revolution than the contribution made by a giant of a man who mysteriously appeared on a dock in City Point, Virginia, in 1765.

According to an eyewitness account, "a foreign
ship sailed up the James River, dropped anchor op-
posite the dock, and lowered a longboat to the water
with two sailors in it. Then a boy of about five years
was handed down and rowed to the wharf, where he
was deposited and abandoned. The boat returned,
quickly, to its ship. The ship weighed anchor at once,
sailed back down the James River, and was never
heard from again."

The boy was well dressed, with silver buckles on his shoes. One buckle formed the initial *P*, and the other the initial *F*. He spoke a combination of European languages, and he was eventually able to communicate to bystanders that his name was Pedro Francisco. According to some accounts, a Portuguese noble named Francisco was being pursued by political enemies, and he orchestrated his son's abduction to protect the boy. Other stories speculate that he was kidnapped by sailors who intended to hold him for ransom or sell him as an indentured servant.

Francisco was shuffled around, moving from seaside warehouses to the county poorhouse, until his story intrigued a local judge named Anthony Winston, who took him in. The judge treated Francisco well and offered the boy all the advantages of someone growing up in a well-to-do household. And grow he did! At a time when the average height of a man was five feet four, Francisco towered over everyone else at the impressive height of six feet six. Remarkably strong, he weighed around 260 pounds.

In 1774 Judge Winston became one of the first Patriot leaders to defy royal authority by participating in illegal legislative sessions. Later he decided to bring fourteen-year-old Peter with him to one of these meetings. Virginia's greatest Revolutionary voices, such as Thomas Jefferson, Richard Henry Lee, and Judge Winston's soon-to-be-famous nephew, Patrick Henry, attended the meeting at St. John's Church in

Richmond. The treasonous topic was armed defiance of British authority, and there Francisco witnessed Patrick Henry give his famous "Give me liberty, or give me death!" speech. Francisco's patriotic fervor was sparked from that moment.

Before the end of the meeting, the convention authorized a Virginia militia, which Francisco wished to join immediately. Judge Winston entreated him to wait a year, which he did. As soon as the year was up, Francisco, age fifteen, eagerly joined the Tenth Virginia as a private. Not long after his enlistment, he saw his first battle and received a minor bullet wound at the Battle of Brandywine Creek. He convalesced at a Quaker home with his new friend, the Marquis de Lafayette.

A month later, Francisco was back in action, defending Philadelphia at the Battle of Germantown and the Siege of Fort Mifflin. He was one of the few who survived to spend the winter of 1777 at Valley Forge. The following summer he was severely wounded at the Battle of Monmouth in New Jersey, and his injuries were so extensive that it took him a year to heal.

Undaunted, he reenlisted and returned under the command of General Washington, where he was one of twenty skilled soldiers selected for the front lines of battle. This group was known as the "forlorn hope," so called because their chances for survival were slim. They were to lead the light infantry assault on Stony Point on the Hudson River, just south of West Point. Peter was the second Patriot soldier to scale the fort's wall, where he engaged in hand-to-hand combat, suffering a nine-inch bayonet gash across his abdomen. He killed three soldiers before capturing the British battle flag. Francisco was one of only four from the "forlorn hope" to survive the assault.

Francisco's enlistment was up shortly after this battle, but he went back and enlisted a third time, then headed south to the next British offensive. Accounts about Francisco's legendary exploits at the Battle of Camden vary somewhat in terms of chronology, but there is no dispute about his bravery on the battlefield.

As the battle intensified, the Patriots' lines broke and American soldiers went into full retreat. Francisco and a few others tried to stem the tide, but eventually they were caught in the chaos. A British dragoon on horseback approached Francisco, his weapon poised to kill him. "Surrender or die!" he shouted.

Francisco responded, "My gun—it isn't even loaded," as he cautiously stood up and extended the musket toward the British soldier. At the last second, Francisco swung it around and impaled the trooper with the bayonet, then lifted the skewered soldier off his horse. Francisco mounted the horse and rode until he encountered more cavalry, which he managed to make his way through by acting like a British sympathizer. Then he spotted his regimental commander, Colonel Mayo, being led away by a British officer. He killed the officer and gave Colonel Mayo the horse he had captured so Mayo could get away.

A second act of heroism at that battle was recognized by the United States Post Office in 1975 with a stamp commemorating Francisco's incredible strength and valor. In the midst of the Patriots' retreat in one battle, Francisco noticed a cannon carriage stuck in the mud. Knowing it would be vulnerable to falling into the hands of the British, he hoisted the 1,100-pound barrel onto his shoulder and carried it to safety.

Several accounts suggest that in recognition for Francisco's outstanding service, George Washington personally had a five-foot-long broadsword made for him. Washington was quoted as saying about Francisco, "Without him we would have lost two crucial battles, perhaps the War, and with it our freedom. He was truly a One Man Army."

Francisco's fourth enlistment landed him in a cavalry unit under the command of Colonel William Washington. Many stories about Francisco's bravery surround his service in the cavalry, but the best known occurred at Guilford Courthouse in 1781. During a single charge, Francisco reportedly killed eleven British guards. An early-American historian named Benson Lossing wrote that later in

★ ★ ★

"Without [Francisco] we would have lost two crucial battles, perhaps the War, and with it our freedom. He was truly a One Man Army."

GEORGE WASHINGTON

the battle a British soldier "pinned Francisco's leg to his horse with a bayonet. . . . [Francisco] assisted the assailant to draw his bayonet forth, when, with terrible force, he brought his broadsword down and cleft the poor fellow's head to his shoulders!"

Francisco continued the attack until he was injured a second time—again by a bayonet in the leg, but this time it slashed him from his knee all the way to his hip. He held on to his horse until he was away from the battle, and then he fainted from the pain. He was left for dead, bleeding profusely, until a Quaker came to his aid and nursed him back to health. For his bravery, Francisco was offered a commission by William Washington, but he refused it due to the fact that he was illiterate.

Having survived five wounds—two of them nearly fatal—Francisco decided his fighting days were over. He enlisted as a scout in what turned out to be the final year of the war. While reconnoitering at a Loyalists' tavern, he was captured by nine British dragoons. There are various accounts of exactly what happened, but most agree that he escaped, leaving several of the nine dragoons dead. Francisco finished his military career by witnessing the surrender of the British at Yorktown.

Finally finished with fighting, the man referred to as George Washington's One-Man Regiment, the Virginia Giant, and the Hercules of the American Revolution directed his passion toward a new pursuit. Her name was Susannah Anderson. Tradition says that Francisco and the Marquis de Lafayette were walking by the same church where Patrick Henry had delivered his famous "Give me liberty!" speech when a lovely girl came down the steps and tripped. The legendary war hero caught her, and he promptly fell in love. There was one glitch, however: Susannah's father objected to him due to his illiteracy. But Francisco wasn't about to let her get away. As one historian put it, "The offer of a commission in William Washington's cavalry hadn't inspired him to try to learn to read and write; but the lure of Susannah Anderson proved a more potent stimulant." After setting up some businesses and putting his nose to the books, Francisco was married to Susannah in 1785.

Francisco's last service to our country was in the Virginia House of Delegates as sergeant at arms, a position he held from 1825 until his death in 1831. Every year on March 15, Peter Francisco Day is celebrated in Virginia, Massachusetts, and Rhode Island to honor Francisco, the mighty defender of life.

JOHN LAURENS

Rebel for the Cause

*From everyone who has been given much, much
will be demanded; and from the one who has been
entrusted with much, much more will be asked.*

LUKE 12:48, NIV

Few colonials had been given as much as John
Laurens, and few gave as much as he did to
the Patriot cause. Son of Henry Laurens, one
of the wealthiest men in the American colonies, John
had every comfort and advantage a man of his period
could have. He was born in Charleston, South Carolina, but sent to Europe for his education. Studying
in Switzerland as a young man, he received the finest
liberal arts education available, one that led him to
believe that all men, including the slaves owned by his
father, had an equal claim to life and liberty.

When the first shots at Lexington were fired,
Laurens was studying law in London. After reading
Thomas Paine's *Common Sense*, which rallied readers
to fight for American independence, Laurens de-
cided, against his father's objections, to return to
America and join the Patriot cause.

Determined to keep his son out of harm's way, Henry Laurens used his considerable influence to secure a position for John as General George Washington's personal assistant. Henry's efforts were largely in vain, however, as John threw himself into action at the Battle of Brandywine on September 11, 1777. The young Marquis de Lafayette, a French aristocrat who fought with the Patriots and was at least as headstrong as John Laurens, said of Laurens that day, "It was not his fault that he was not killed or wounded; he did everything that was necessary to procure one or t'other."

Laurens proved to be as bullheaded off the battlefield as he was on it. While serving as Washington's assistant, Laurens was aware of the great contribution free blacks from New England were making to the Revolution. Given the Patriots' dire need for soldiers and the large number of enslaved blacks in the South, Laurens advanced a plan to arm slaves and grant them freedom in exchange for military service. The initiative would have been bold in its own right, and it was even more so coming from the son of one of the most prominent slaveholders in the American colonies.

Laurens argued the plan's merits forcefully to

★ ★ ★

"It was not his fault that he was not killed or wounded; [Laurens] did everything that was necessary to procure one or t'other."

THE MARQUIS DE LAFAYETTE

anyone who would listen, including Alexander Hamilton, George Washington, and even his own father. In a letter to his father in 1778, likely sent when Henry was president of the Continental Congress, Laurens wrote,

> I had barely hinted to you, my dearest Father, my desire to augment the Continental Forces from an untried Source. . . . [The raising of black battalions would] advance those who are unjustly deprived of the Rights of Mankind . . . [and] reinforce the Defenders of Liberty with a number of gallant Soldiers.

Though Laurens's plan fell on some sympathetic ears, he still faced an uphill challenge in winning approval in the face of strong Southern opposition. But that didn't faze him.

He took his proposal directly to Congress, and his effective persuasion led to this congressional resolution:

> That it be recommended to the states of South Carolina and Georgia, if they shall think the same expedient, to take measures immediately for raising three thousand able-bodied negroes.

Laurens's integrity was evident not only in his fight for equality but also in his loyalty to his leaders. Given the ebbs and flows of the war, there was no shortage of criticism for General Washington's leadership. Several officers, most notably General Thomas Conway, began suggesting that Washington was not fit to command the Continental Army and that someone like General Horatio Gates, who had recently won a stunning victory over the British at Saratoga, New York, was better equipped to lead the fight. As Washington's personal aide, Laurens felt duty bound to aggressively combat what came to be known as the Conway Cabal. Laurens wrote eloquently in defense of Washington to his father, confirming Henry's already-positive view of Washington and strengthening Washington's political position in the Continental Congress.

Laurens was not a man of half measures when it came to fighting for what he believed in. When General Charles Lee, who was considered Washington's second-in-command and had just been court-martialed, made some vicious remarks against Washington, Laurens took the unusual step of challenging Lee to a duel. At the time, dueling was a tolerated, though increasingly frowned-upon, means of addressing attacks on someone's honor.

The severity of the offense dictated the conduct of the duel. Duelers usually marched away from each other before turning and firing. The more serious the offense, the closer the duelers stood when they fired. In this instance, Lee and Laurens actually faced each other at the beginning of the duel and marched *toward* each other, until they were within six paces. They both fired. Lee's shot missed; Laurens's shot grazed Lee. The disgraced general insisted on another shot, and Laurens accepted. Their seconds, present to make sure the rules were upheld and to attempt reconciliation after the duel, insisted that honor had been satisfied, and both men withdrew. Laurens's willingness to lay down his life for a verbal offense toward his commander left an impression on Lee, who admitted later that he'd gained an "odd sort of respect for [Laurens]."

If standing up to a general wasn't enough to convince people of Laurens's righteous bravery, then his conduct toward the king of France removed all doubt. Congress sent Laurens to France to assist the American minister, Benjamin Franklin, in securing money and supplies from the French Crown. After waiting restlessly for weeks, Laurens directly petitioned King Louis XVI, against the counsel of Franklin, at a reception where individuals were only permitted to pay their respects and bow. Quite possibly putting his life, but also his country's survival, on the line, he informed the king, in an exchange that may be apocryphal but certainly not uncharacteristic, that "should the favor asked be denied, or even delayed, there is cause to fear that the sword which I wear may no longer be drawn in defense of the liberties of my country, but be wielded as a British subject against the monarchy of France."

Laurens did not have to wait much longer before he was sent back to America, accompanied by two ships filled with military goods and half a million dollars.

As the war wound down, many recognized Laurens's political potential. Alexander Hamilton, writing to Laurens after Hamilton secured a position in the Continental Congress, implored Laurens, in a letter dated August 15, 1782, to "quit your sword, my friend. . . . Come to Congress. We know each other's sentiments, our views are the same; we have fought side by side to make America free, let us hand in hand struggle to make her happy."

Laurens never had a chance to realize his peacetime potential. On August 27, 1782, Laurens and his men were ambushed by 140 British soldiers. Despite being outnumbered three to one, Laurens refused to surrender or retreat, leading a charge that earned him a volley of musket balls. He dropped from his horse, mortally wounded.

His father was devastated. This slave owner ended up honoring his son the best way he knew how—by arranging for the freedom of all 260 family slaves, as his son, the advocate of the right to life and freedom for all, had requested.

Of John Laurens, Washington wrote, "In a word, he had not a fault that I ever could discover, unless intrepidity [i.e., boldness] bordering upon rashness could come under that denomination; and to this he was excited by the purest motives."

Engraved on Laurens's tombstone on his family's plantation along the Cooper River is a sentiment he carried within his soul and lived out through his bold and heroic actions:

Dulce et decorum est pro patria mori.
(*Sweet and fitting it is to die for one's country.*)

AUSTIN DABNEY

The Substitute

★ ★ ★

*Never abandon a friend—either yours or your father's. When
disaster strikes, you won't have to ask your brother for assistance.
It's better to go to a neighbor than to a brother who lives far away.*

PROVERBS 27:10, NLT

The great blemish on our country in the Revolutionary War era was that so many Americans, primarily in the South, continued to embrace the institution of slavery, which denied blacks the right to govern their own lives. Though the Declaration of Independence declared that all men were created equal and had equal claim to their inherent rights, our country denied a large portion of the population the free exercise of those rights.

But even in the most ardent of slave states, there were signs of hope during the period of the Revolution. One such sign can be found today in a cemetery in Pike County, Georgia. A tombstone there reads:

Austin Dabney
Georgia Militia

Revolutionary War
Freed Slave
Devoted Friend to Harris Family

The marker is a summary of the remarkable story of the Georgian slave Austin Dabney and his personal journey from slavery to freedom.

Austin Dabney was born a slave, raised a slave, and even fought for the Patriots as a slave. His master, Richard Aycock, a resident of Wilkes County, Georgia, had no interest in fighting for the Patriots himself, so he sent a willing Dabney to the Georgia militia as his substitute.

Dabney saw action in one of Georgia's bloodiest Revolutionary War engagements, the Battle of Kettle Creek, and may have been the only black man who served among the Patriots in that battle. During the battle, he suffered a severe injury to his thigh—an injury that could have been life threatening but turned out to be a life-changing opportunity. One of his fellow soldiers, Giles Harris, took him to a nearby home to treat his wound. Harris regarded this injured man not as a slave, not as an inferior being, but as a brother in arms. Over time, Harris and Dabney formed a friendship that defied racial prejudices and transcended the racial boundaries of colonial Georgia.

Not much is known about Dabney's life over the next seven years. He remained a slave but had clearly earned the respect and admiration of Harris and his fellow soldiers. On August 14, 1786, the Georgia legislature saw fit not only to authorize the payment of up to seventy pounds for Dabney's emancipation but also to grant him fifty acres of land. This made Dabney the only black man in the state of Georgia to receive a land grant for his military service. Of Dabney, the legislature wrote,

> During the revolution, instead of advantaging himself of the times to withdraw himself from the American lines and enter with the majority of his color and fellow slaves in the service of his Britannic majesty and his officers and vassals, [Dabney] did voluntarily enroll himself in some one of the Corps under the command of Colonel Elijah Clarke, and in several actions and engagements behaved against the common enemy with a bravery and fortitude which would have honored a freeman, and in one of which engagements he was severely wounded, and rendered incapable of hard servitude; and policy as well as gratitude demand a return for such services and behavior from the Commonwealth.

★ ★ ★

"[Dabney] behaved against the common enemy with a bravery and fortitude which would have honored a freeman."

GEORGIA LEGISLATURE

George Gilmer, an early Georgia governor and historian, said of Dabney, "No soldier under [Clarke] was braver, or did better service during the revolutionary struggle."

The legislature authorized Colonel Clarke, along with two others, to negotiate the emancipation price with Aycock. Clarke was eager to vouch for Dabney's service to the cause, and Dabney's freedom was secured. Starting in 1789, the federal government also awarded Dabney a military pension of sixty dollars a year, which rose to ninety-six dollars a year in 1816.

With his land secured and a strong work ethic, Dabney made a decent living for himself. He never forgot the kindness Giles Harris had showed him, and he treated Harris and his family as if they were his own. The feeling was clearly mutual, as Giles named his son William Dabney Harris.

As William Harris reached maturity, he dreamed of going to college, but the Harris family, for reasons unknown, did not provide the funds for him to continue his schooling. Dabney stepped in and paid for William's tuition at Franklin College, which later became the University of Georgia. Dabney's support did not end there. He assisted William financially throughout his time in college and then while William was studying to become a lawyer under attorney Stephen Upson in Lexington, Georgia.

The love and care bestowed on a white family from a former slave made a lasting impression on Upson—one that compelled him to take an unpopular position on behalf of Dabney in later years, when Upson served as a state legislator in Georgia. In the early 1800s, Georgia conducted a series of land lotteries that gave residents the opportunity to buy large parcels of land in the state's interior at dirt-cheap prices. The chances for getting this opportunity rose significantly for those who had served in the military. As a black man, Dabney was not permitted to participate in any of the lotteries, despite the fact that he was a Patriot veteran. Upson thought the state's position was unjust, and he sponsored a resolution that, rather than offering Dabney an opportunity to purchase land, actually granted him an additional 112 acres of land for his service to the state.

Dabney would stay close to the Harris family, literally, for the rest of his life. He followed them to three different counties before finally settling in Pike County, where he passed away in 1830. Dabney left all his material goods to the Harris family, who buried him in their family plot in Pike County.

Perhaps the clearest indication that the Harris family's regard for Dabney was as strong as Dabney's for them came five years later, when William Harris named his newborn son Austin Dabney Harris. And just before William passed away, as the story goes, his last request was that his body be laid in death next to the man he regarded as his best friend in life: Austin Dabney.

THOMAS NELSON JR.

The Virginian
Signer of the Declaration of Independence

★ ★ ★

Do not love the world or anything in the world. . . . For everything
in the world—the lust of the flesh, the lust of the eyes, and the pride of
life—comes not from the Father but from the world. The world and
its desires pass away, but whoever does the will of God lives forever.

1 JOHN 2:15-17, NIV

S ome Patriots sacrificed fortunes for the cause, some offered their lives and their health in the military, and some risked their safety by signing the Declaration of Independence. Thomas Nelson Jr. did it all.

Nelson was born in 1738 in his father's mansion in Yorktown, Virginia. Nelson's grandfather, a merchant of great reputation, had settled in Yorktown in the early 1700s. As was common for the wealthy of that time, young Thomas was sent to a private school in London at age fourteen. He remained in England and went on to earn a degree at Cambridge. In 1761, at age twenty-two, he returned to Virginia.

Though he enjoyed his years of education in Europe, his time in England did not make him sympathetic to British tyranny in the colonies. He closely observed the restrictive actions of the British king and Parliament until 1774, when he decided to take a stand. He started by sending much-needed supplies to besieged Boston. He also helped start Yorktown's own tea party, during which he personally threw chests of tea into the river, following the trend the Bostonians had started. Nelson was also elected to the Virginia House of Burgesses, along with many other famous Patriots.

When the British dissolved the assembly in an attempt to further limit American freedom, Nelson joined a group of Patriots who held unauthorized legislative meetings. In one session Nelson was the bold one who proposed the treasonous legislation that authorized the formation of a state militia. An ardent supporter of bearing arms, Nelson offered these passionate words in one of his speeches:

> I am a merchant of Yorktown, but I am a Virginian first. Let my trade perish. I call God to witness that if any British troops are landed in the County of York, of which I am Lieutenant, I will wait no orders, but will summon the militia and drive the invaders into the sea!

Nelson's rhetoric earned him an appointment as colonel in the Virginia military. He resigned his commission a year later due to a new directive: his appointment to the Second Continental Congress, replacing the famous Patrick Henry. Nelson served as an outspoken supporter of the Declaration of Independence, voting for it in Congress and then signing it.

A year after the Declaration was signed, Nelson became ill and seemed to lose his memory from the sickness. At the urging of his friends and colleagues, Nelson withdrew from Congress, despite his unwillingness to leave his post. He went back to Yorktown, but he didn't remain inactive for long. Soon the British fleet was just off the Virginia coast, and the state chose him to command the Virginia militia in its defense. The fleet ended up invading Philadelphia instead of Virginia, so newly appointed Brigadier General Nelson personally raised money (much of it from his own pocket) to form a volunteer corps. Under his command, the volunteer troops went to Philadelphia to aid General Washington, though they never saw action before returning to Virginia.

As it turned out, the expedition aided Nelson's health—so much so that by 1779 he seemed fully recovered and able to serve his country as a delegate again, sitting on several committees in the Continental Congress. Unfortunately, while serving in Congress, his ailment returned and he began struggling with his memory again. Once more he resigned and returned home to recover.

As his health improved and as Virginia became the central theater for war, Nelson was called back to military action. British forces had marched from the south and ravaged lower Virginia, and the state was also facing attacks on the coast from a small British flotilla. As if it weren't enough to serve as the head of the Virginia forces, General Nelson was asked to step into another significant role. Thomas Jefferson's term as governor had just expired as the British campaign swept into Virginia, and Nelson was elected by popular vote to take Jefferson's place. Somehow he was able to continue commanding the state militia while simultaneously running the government.

Through personal devotion and his own financial contributions, Nelson was able to keep his troops together, and they fought heroically at the Siege of Yorktown. Accounts of what happened at that battle vary somewhat, but what is known is that General Nelson and his troops served with distinction. In fact, General Washington made honorable mention of them in a letter:

> The magnitude of the acquisition will be ample compensation for the difficulties and dangers which they met with so much firmness and patriotism.

"Entertaining the most ardent love for civil and religious liberty, [Nelson] was among the first of that glorious band of patriots whose exertions dashed and defeated the machinations of British tyranny."

COLONEL JAMES INNES

One story from the Siege of Yorktown highlights just how committed Nelson was to the cause. Nelson is said to have noticed that his home, the Nelson House, had not been shelled—probably out of respect for him. He also understood that General Cornwallis, the commander of the British troops, had turned Nelson's home into their central command. Some accounts say that Nelson entreated General Washington to shell the house; others say he went to the Marquis de Lafayette, requesting that the French bombard it. Still another account says that, as commander of the Virginia militia, Nelson personally ordered it shelled by his own men. Whatever the case, this Patriot was willing to sacrifice his own interests for the good of the greater cause.

A month after the American victory over Cornwallis at Yorktown, Governor Nelson took ill again. This time it was serious enough that he resigned from serving as governor and commander of the militia. He never recovered and was no longer able to participate in public life. Thomas Nelson Jr. passed away in January 1789 and was buried at the Grace Episcopal Church in Yorktown, directly across the street from his ancestral home.

Nelson unselfishly dedicated his life and his health to the American cause. One of his fellow officers, Colonel James Innes, wrote these words in memory of Nelson:

As a man, a citizen, a legislator, and a patriot, he exhibited a conduct untarnished and undebased by sordid or selfish interest, and strongly marked with the genuine characteristics of true religion, sound benevolence, and liberal policy. Entertaining the most ardent love for civil and religious liberty, he was among the first of that glorious band of patriots whose exertions dashed and defeated the machinations of British tyranny, and gave United America freedom and independent empire.

JAMES ARMISTEAD LAFAYETTE, LYDIA DARRAGH, AND NATHAN HALE

The Spies

Many claim to have unfailing love, but a faithful person who can find?
PROVERBS 20:6, NIV

P atriots who bore arms against the British always faced the possibility of death on the battlefield. They also faced the threat that, if captured by the British, they would be confined as prisoners of war until a prisoner exchange or liberation at the end of the war. Those engaged as spies, however, knew that they would never see the walls of a prison if they were caught. Their punishment would be the hangman's noose or some other equally lethal sentence.

While soldiers tended to fit a certain general mold, spies came in every shape, size, and gender. During the war, there were "professional spies" who gathered information as their contribution to the cause. More often, though, spies were soldiers who volunteered for a particular mission or civilians who found espionage a way to fight without donning a uniform.

When James Armistead, a slave from Virginia, asked his master's permission to join the Patriot cause, he likely never dreamed he would become a spy, much less play a key role in one of the decisive battles of the war. He wanted to fight because he was looking for an opportunity to prove that his own life was worth more than servitude to another person.

One of General Washington's most trusted aides, the French nobleman Marquis de Lafayette, advised him that acquiring the assistance of black men would greatly help the army—not just by providing needed laborers, but also in combating the British cavalry advantage. According to Lafayette, "Nothing but a treaty of alliance with the Negroes can find us dragoon Horses [because] it is by this means the enemy have so formidable a Cavalry." Armistead joined the service under this initiative by Lafayette and quickly proved himself invaluable to the Patriot cause.

The British relied heavily on American blacks for intelligence about Patriot movements. This prompted Lafayette to employ Armistead as a disinformation agent, in which role he pretended to feed British general Charles Cornwallis intelligence that would compromise the Americans. In doing so, he gave the Patriots a tactical advantage that helped them pin Cornwallis and his men at Yorktown. Armistead had been such an effective spy that it was only after Cornwallis's surrender in Yorktown, when the defeated general found Armistead in Lafayette's headquarters, that he realized he had been duped.

In recognition of Armistead's faithful and exemplary service, Lafayette offered the following testimonial, which aided Virginia in its decision to emancipate Armistead for his service:

> This is to certify that the bearer by the name of James has done essential services to me while I had the honour to command in this state. His intelligences from the enemy's camp were industriously collected and faithfully delivered. He perfectly acquitted himself with some important commissions I gave him and appears to me entitled to every reward his situation can admit of.

Grateful to Lafayette for his regard, Armistead changed his name to James Armistead Lafayette and lived out the rest of his years as a free man. Lafayette himself spent many years after the war in a Prussian prison, having alienated both royalists and radicals during the political upheaval in Europe. When the general made his triumphal return to the United States almost forty years later, he reportedly spotted James in a crowd and embraced his former comrade and namesake.

Like James Armistead Lafayette, Lydia Darragh was a spy who risked her life for the cause of her country. And for her the stakes were even higher: her espionage could have expelled her from membership in her pacifist Quaker sect. During the war, Darragh, an Irish immigrant, secretly came to support the Patriot cause, but in keeping with her Quaker beliefs, she was careful to stay publicly neutral and oppose any violent actions. Her eldest son, however, defied the Quakers' pacifist stance and joined the Patriot army.

When the British army moved into Philadelphia, British troops were looking for a building to conduct operational meetings. They deemed the Darragh home to be a prime location and moved to evict her and her family. On her way to appeal the eviction to British general William Howe, she fortuitously ran into a British captain who happened to be a second cousin of hers from Ireland. The captain intervened, allowing the Darragh family to stay in their home, provided they kept a room available for British officers to meet in.

On the night of December 2, 1777, the British forced the Darraghs to stay in their bedrooms while they conducted a secret meeting. Fearful of what the British were plotting, Darragh sneaked into a closet next to the meeting room and discovered they were planning a surprise attack on December 4 against General Washington's army at nearby Whitemarsh, where her son was stationed.

Despite the risks, Darragh knew she had no choice but to devise a way to warn Washington's army and protect her son. Knowing the penalty for espionage, she kept her plan secret from everyone—even her husband and younger son. She received permission from General Howe to leave Philadelphia under the pretext of getting flour at a nearby mill and visiting her two youngest children, whom she had previously sent out of the city for their protection. Early on December 4, she trudged through several miles of snow on her way to the Rising Sun Tavern, a place known for transmitting colonial messages. According to an account by her daughter Ann, before Darragh arrived at the tavern, she encountered Thomas Craig, a member of Pennsylvania's Patriot militia, and he successfully conveyed her warning to Washington.

A report from Colonel Elias Boudinot relates a slightly different account. According to Boudinot, a woman who appears to have been Darragh approached him at the tavern on December 4 and surreptitiously handed him a needle book. Boudinot later reflected on her message:

> General Howe was coming out the next morning with 5,000 men, 13 pieces of cannon, baggage wagons, and 11 [boats] on wheels. On comparing this with other information, I found it true and immediately rode post to headquarters.

Whichever account is true, the fact remains that Washington was able to respond in time to thwart the British, thanks to some confidential information he received. British spymaster John Andre, the man who recruited Benedict Arnold from the Patriots, went to the Darragh home to determine if one of the Darraghs could have leaked the plans. Lydia convinced him that everyone had been asleep early the night of the meeting. Befuddled, Andre reportedly said, "One thing is certain: the enemy had notice of our coming, were prepared for us, and we marched back like a parcel of fools. The walls must have ears." Indeed.

The most famous spy of the war failed at spying, but he still managed to inspire a nation with his sacrificial love of country. Nathan Hale was raised by prosperous farmers and devout Puritans in Coventry, Connecticut. Hale applied the industrious habits of his parents to his studies at Yale College and graduated at the age of eighteen, taking a teaching position at the Union Grammar School in New London, Connecticut.

As a prominent young man whose career was just beginning to take off, Hale appeared to hold back at first when the fighting broke out between the British and the colonists. Several months later, Hale received a letter from his former classmate Benjamin Tallmadge, dated July 4, 1775. In it Tallmadge acknowledged that Hale was certainly performing a great public service in the classroom but declared that were he in Hale's shoes, "the more extensive Service would be my choice. Our holy Religion, the honour of our God, a glorious country, & a happy constitution is what we have to defend."

The next day, having decided to commit himself fully to the cause, Hale joined the Seventh Connecticut Regiment as a first lieutenant. The young Patriot soon proved he would do anything that was asked of him. Hale accepted command of a company in the country's first special forces unit, the New England Rangers. General Washington, attempting to defend Manhattan in the summer of 1776, desperately needed intelligence about where the British were going to attack. Hale, despite his lack of experience in espionage, volunteered to sneak behind enemy lines on Long Island. He risked not only death if he were caught but also his reputation, since spying was considered dishonorable by many at the time, especially among people of Hale's higher station. Hale nevertheless told his good friend William Hull upon accepting the assignment, "I wish to be useful, and every kind of service necessary for the public good, becomes honorable by being necessary. If the exigencies of my country demand a peculiar service, its claims to the performance of that service are imperious."

Hull, who later became a Revolutionary general, did everything he could to talk Hale out of spying, pointing out that Hale was too honest to do the kind of lying necessary to be a good spy. Hale insisted that he had to do something for his country, no matter how dangerous. He was keenly aware that his fellow soldiers were suffering because they didn't know British plans and, therefore, could not properly prepare for their attacks.

The second week of September, Hale crossed enemy lines, allegedly in the guise of a Connecticut schoolmaster looking to find employment. The British invaded Manhattan shortly after Hale began his mission, but he continued to gather what intelligence he could. About a week later, Hale was on his way back to report his findings when the British captured him. One report suggests that a Loyalist cousin betrayed him, knowing full well the kind of punishment Hale would face. Once detained, he was searched, and several documents hidden in his shoe soles confirmed him as a spy.

Hull was right about Hale not being a good liar—in fact, he didn't even attempt to deny his true identity, giving his captors his name and rank. British general William Howe sentenced Hale to hang the next day.

Hale requested to meet with a clergyman and be given a Bible, but the British denied him that consolation—something unheard of in that time, even for enemies. This story spread like wildfire among the Americans, further fueling their anger toward the British. British engineer John Montresor, watching over Hale in the hours leading up to his execution, was moved by the young man's composure, as well as his final, immortalized lament: "I only regret that I have but one life to lose for my country."

Those words could easily be echoed by the other spies of the Revolution, all of whom were willing to risk their lives for this cause they so fervently believed in.

★ ★ ★

"I only regret that I have but one life
to lose for my country."

NATHAN HALE

I suspect if you asked Americans what one quality or concept makes the United States stand apart from other countries, the overwhelming response would be freedom or liberty. They would, of course, be correct. No people in the history of the world have enjoyed more freedom than Americans have over the past two centuries.

Life is the foundational right listed in our Declaration of Independence, and happiness is the aspiration to be pursued. Our founders viewed liberty as the state that must exist for man to be able to realize that pursuit.

Although freedom is universally valued in our country, many Americans have a difficult time defining what it really means. In my experience, most people define freedom as the absence of constraints—an environment where individuals can do what they want to do. I suspect that since the words *liberty* and *freedom* are interchangeable today, liberty would be defined in much the same way.

The definition of freedom has held constant

since our founding. In the first American dictionary, published by Noah Webster thirty years after the signing of the Declaration of Independence, freedom was defined as "a state of exemption from the power or control of another; exemption from slavery, servitude or confinement." Freedom is, in other words, an environment where people can do what they want to do!

Webster's original dictionary definition of liberty is rich and complex, making it distinct from both his definition of freedom and today's definition of liberty. Not surprisingly, the first definition of liberty focuses on "freedom from restraint, in a general sense, and applicable to the body, or to the will or mind." But Webster doesn't just describe liberty in terms of "freedom from"; he also refers to *natural liberty*, expanding the definition to include "freedom to." He defines natural liberty as "the power of acting as one thinks fit, without any restraint or control, except from the laws of nature." So liberty is not just the removal of constraints but also the positive ability to act freely, limited only by natural law. This limitation on liberty is critical because ultimately it is the only way to ensure liberty for all.

Webster elaborates on the definition of liberty as it relates to society as a whole. He uses the term *civil liberty* and defines it as "natural liberty, so far only abridged and restrained, as is necessary and expedient for the safety and interest of the society." In order for liberty to be achieved for the individual, there must be legal or societal restraints on the individual. So the liberty our founders contemplated was not a simplistic "freedom from" the power and control of others. In fact, liberty requires some constraint on people's "freedom to" do what they want to do—if that action has a detrimental impact on the liberty of others and on society.

However, I believe our founders had an even more complete understanding of liberty than Webster's "freedom from" and "freedom to . . . as long as no one else gets hurt." They proposed the kind of liberty that they believed was necessary to foster not just a great and powerful nation but also a good and virtuous people. They advanced a definition of liberty that included a "freedom *for*."

It is clear from our founders' writings that the liberty they envisioned was not a freedom to do whatever one wants to do but a freedom to do what one *ought* to do according to "the Laws of Nature and of Nature's God." Our founders believed in natural law, in self-evident truths, in right and wrong. They knew that unless Americans lived virtuous lives, liberty would be fleeting.

The author Os Guinness describes the interrelationship between virtue, faith, and freedom as the "golden triangle of freedom." Freedom requires virtue, virtue requires faith, and faith requires freedom—and then it goes around again.

Without virtue, disorder will result, leading to more government control and therefore less freedom. Theoretically, virtue can exist without faith, but in practice faith is the only way to instill virtue on a mass scale across a society, as we have seen here in the United States. And for faith to propagate throughout the country, freedom of conscience is necessary. As such, these concepts work together to ensure liberty.

There was no concept that inspired the men and women of the Revolution more than liberty. The Patriots in this section longed for liberty and put their lives, their fortunes, and their sacred honor on the line to secure it for themselves and their posterity.

NANCY MORGAN HART

War Woman

Don't imagine that I came to bring peace to the earth!
I came not to bring peace, but a sword.

MATTHEW 10:34, NLT

Among the Patriots of the American Revolution, there are heroes and there are larger-than-life heroes. And then there is Nancy Morgan Hart. A gutsy woman whose bold, take-no-prisoners persona has inspired patriots for generations, she possessed the backbone necessary to stand up to the British, fight for her liberties, and not back down, even in the face of mortal danger.

Growing up in North Carolina, Nancy became an accomplished frontierswoman, developing skills as an herbalist and an expert sharpshooter. Her fearlessness and hair-trigger temper helped earn her the nickname War Woman from local Cherokees.

Nancy married Benjamin Hart when she was

thirty-six, an unusually late age for a woman of that period to marry. Shortly after their nuptials, the Harts moved to the Wilkes River area in northern Georgia.

People who knew Nancy Hart reportedly had some colorful and complex descriptions of her. Apparently she was a striking sight. At a time when women were barely five feet tall on average, Hart stood six feet tall, with a masculine frame and flaming red hair. She was alternately labeled "vulgar and illiterate" along with "hospitable and valorous." According to one record, she didn't turn too many heads, "a fact she herself would have readily acknowledged, had she ever enjoyed an opportunity of looking into a mirror."

In spite of her age, she and her husband had eight children—six sons and two daughters. Though Nancy was more renowned than her husband, he seems to have earned a solid reputation for himself as well. Once the war began, Benjamin served as a lieutenant in the Georgia militia. Though little is known of the particulars of his service, he made a significant-enough contribution to earn a gift of twenty bushels of corn in 1781 from the Georgia Executive Council to help provide for his family.

Although women did not serve in the military, Nancy soon distinguished herself as "a honey of a Patriot." Despite having to tend to her children alone while her husband was off fighting, she found time to engage in some creative espionage. In January 1778 she disguised herself as a man, which, considering her build, was not too difficult, and ventured into Augusta, Georgia, to gather information on the British defenses. In addition to her masculine appearance, she portrayed herself as a dim-witted person, thus deflecting any suspicion. She also reportedly "wandered" into several other Loyalist and British camps, gathering valuable information for the Patriots. (The CIA has highlighted her work as an effective use of disguise in the Revolutionary War.)

Hart is probably best known, though, for taking on the British on her own property. As one story goes, a British spy came up to her cabin and peered through a crack in the outside wall. One of Hart's children could see the spy's eye through the crack and quietly informed her mother, who was standing at the fireplace, making soap. Hart filled her ladle with boiling, soapy water and quickly flipped it through the crack. Screaming and immobilized, the spy was putty in her hands as she tied him up and handed him over to the Patriot militia.

That incident was just a warm-up for one of the most famous British takedowns by any Patriot. Late one day, British soldiers showed up at Hart's cabin while her husband was working in one of their fields. They demanded to know the whereabouts of a Patriot leader who had just come by her home asking for assistance. She brazenly told the soldiers she hadn't seen anyone pass by her cabin in days. Suspecting she was being less than truthful, the soldiers decided to put her in her place. They shot one of her turkeys and ordered her to cook the bird for them on the spot. They also demanded something to drink.

Outwardly obliging, Hart poured them wine. When the soldiers had drunk enough to feel a little more comfortable, Hart sent her daughter outside, presumably to fetch some water. In reality, however, she was to signal her father. As Hart was serving the soldiers, she slowly and stealthily began to slip their muskets, which they had stacked in a corner, out through a small opening in the cabin wall to her daughter. As she was about to move the third musket, though, the soldiers suddenly realized what she was doing and jumped to their feet. Not missing a beat, Hart swung the musket around, pointed it at the soldiers, and threatened to shoot the first man who made a move. One soldier was either hard of hearing or severely underestimated her. He jumped toward her, and she shot him dead.

Hart quickly picked up another loaded musket and held the rest of the soldiers at gunpoint until her husband arrived with several militiamen. Benjamin thought they should simply shoot them all. Not Nancy. Shooting was too good for these redcoats; she wanted them to hang. So they strung up the five remaining soldiers on a nearby tree.

More than 130 years later, workers putting in

★ ★ ★

"[Hart] . . . became a shouting Christian, [and] fought the Devil as manfully as she had [once] fought the Tories."

GEORGIA GOVERNOR GEORGE GILMER

a railroad through the old Hart property made an unusual discovery. As they were grading the land, they found a neat row of skeletons, six of them, buried under three feet of earth.

Hart was a woman of uncommon fire and courage whose legacy has lived on through the generations. Her nephew was Henry Clay, three-term Speaker of the House of Representatives and Secretary of State under President John Quincy Adams. Another relation was Senator Thomas Hart Benton of Missouri, who was a strong advocate of westward expansion and became the first senator to serve five terms.

During the Civil War, some Confederate women decided to form their own militia, and they named themselves the Nancy Harts. Hart has a city, a lake, a highway, and a county named after her in Georgia. Right near where her old cabin stood, the Daughters of the American Revolution have reconstructed a replica of the cabin, incorporating the original chimney stones that once bore witness to the day a frontierswoman held her ground in the battle for freedom.

ABRAHAM WHIPPLE, JONATHAN HARADEN, AND LAMBERT WICKES

The Privateers

★ ★ ★

*If I rise on the wings of the dawn, if I settle on the far side of the sea,
even there your hand will guide me, your right hand will hold me fast.*

PSALM 139:9-10, NIV

Ralph Waldo Emerson penned the words "the shot heard round the world" to describe the beginning of the Revolutionary War in Lexington and Concord, Massachusetts. However, the sound that got the drums of war beating in the colonies even before that was a shot fired in Rhode Island—three years before Lexington. The engagement known as the *Gaspée* Affair was one of many lesser-known battles that pitted the feeble colonial naval forces against the great British navy. Despite their relative obscurity, these naval engagements and the men who led them made a significant contribution to the war effort. Although the naval battles did not result in as many casualties as the large land battles, the Patriots at sea accomplished some equally heroic feats. Considering how significantly outgunned the Americans were, they performed with commendable bravery and tenacity.

The attack on the British schooner *Gaspée* came in response to the imposition of taxes and import duties by the British, which they were demanding to help pay for the Seven Years' War. This enraged American sailors. One of them, Abraham Whipple, led a group of disgruntled sailors to take vengeance on the *Gaspée*, which had been tasked with pursuing colonial ships to collect taxes. Someone shot the king's revenue officer, and the other crew members were surrounded and taken to shore. The Americans then boarded the *Gaspée* and burned it.

Despite his leadership in this event and his heroic battles at sea, Whipple's reputation has faded over the years. He has been called the "forgotten man of the Continental Navy." Although he was well known in his day, today Whipple has hardly more than a book written about him and a few Rhode Island streets named in his honor.

Abraham Whipple was born in Providence, Rhode Island, to a farmer, but he was quickly drawn

"Being chased into the Harbor by four British Ships of War, we then sent our whole force and strained every nerve for the defense of the Town."

ABRAHAM WHIPPLE

to life at sea. As a young man, he became captain of a merchant ship that voyaged from New England to the West Indies. From this experience he gained knowledge of the sea and various ports that would become invaluable during the Revolution. He then became a privateer for the British during the French and Indian War, commanding the *Game Cock*, which reportedly captured dozens of French ships for Britain.

When Rhode Island formed the first American navy during the Revolution, Abraham Whipple was commissioned as commodore of the *Katy* as well as a little boat called the *Washington*. He was in command during the first official naval battle for the Americans, firing on and capturing the British *Diana*. As the war progressed, Whipple exchanged missives with Sir James Wallace, commander of the British *Rose*. Once Wallace wrote to Whipple, threatening to have the American hanged for the *Gaspée* Affair and for bruising his ego in a number of sneaky naval actions. In response, Whipple simply wrote, "Always catch a man before you hang him."

Commodore Whipple and his ships were soon transferred from Rhode Island to the Continental Navy, and one of his ships was renamed the *Providence*. The Continental Navy gave Whipple command of several other ships as well. Whipple took his vessels on numerous excursions on behalf of the colonies— along the East Coast, to the Bahamas, and toward Newfoundland. On his mission north, his armada captured more than a million dollars' worth of ships and cargo for the American cause—largely thought to be one of the richest captures of the war. Amazingly, in all these engagements, Whipple was said never to have fired a shot. One of his favorite tactics was to fool enemy ships into thinking his ship was friendly—hiding his guns and running up the British flag so he could close in and then demand surrender.

Whipple, with some of the only available Continental naval vessels, was ordered to go to Charleston, South Carolina, to harass the British forces just starting their southern campaign. Unfortunately, he went up a river that turned out to be a trap. The Americans were unable to break out, and the British captured or sank all of Whipple's ships. Whipple was taken captive and held as a prisoner of war.

After his release, Whipple returned home to his wife and two daughters to find that their debts had accumulated while he was away. Unable to secure the back pay he was owed for his time at sea, he eventually had to mortgage his farm. In 1784, in an effort to get money, Whipple set out on a commercial cruise to England. The excursion was a financial failure, but it ended up succeeding on another level. When he entered the port of London after the Revolutionary War, it turned out that his vessel was the first ship to unfurl the American flag there.

Jonathan Haraden was a merchant ship captain when the war began, and like many other seamen, he answered the call to defend freedom by joining the small Massachusetts navy. He took part in several important sea battles on the *Tyrannicide* and eventually was promoted to captain of the ship. But Haraden's real claim to fame came from privateering for the American government. Given the limited resources of the Continental Congress, a regular navy of any size was out of the question, so privateers provided the much-needed force that kept the British occupied at sea.

Haraden's seafaring talent and reckless streak made him well suited for privateering. In 1780 he took command of forty-five men and boys on the fourteen-gun *General Pickering* and headed toward Europe. When Haraden reached the Bay of Biscay near Spain, he spotted a British privateer, the *Golden Eagle*, and decided to capture her. Under the cover of darkness, he pulled up beside the ship and yelled that he was commanding an American frigate (but in reality, his vessel was much smaller). He threatened the British captain, who surrendered instantly. Haraden didn't realize that another British ship lurked in the harbor—the *Achilles*, which was three times the size of the *General Pickering*. No matter. Two days later Haraden took it on anyway, as hundreds of people watched from the shoreline. The two ships battled for hours until the British finally fled.

In his most famous engagement, Haraden took on a much larger British mail ship heading toward England. At the climax of the battle, the American sailors realized they had only enough gunpowder for one last broadside. When the crew informed Haraden, he calmly said that was fine and ordered the guns to be loaded. Audacious almost to a fault, he sailed up beside the other ship and threatened to shoot and sink her if the captain didn't surrender in five minutes. The bluff worked, and the outwitted British surrendered to Haraden.

By the end of the war, Haraden had captured more than one thousand cannons in addition to countless weapons, goods, and supplies. His bold tactics, as well as his coolness under fire, made him one of the Revolution's greatest naval heroes. In an act of tribute to the legendary captain, the United States Navy built a destroyer during World War I named after Haraden. In an ironic twist, it was given to the British in World War II.

Lambert Wickes was another commander in the Continental Navy during the Revolution. One of his first missions after being given command of the sixteen-gun brig *Reprisal* was to sail to the West Indies and get munitions for the army. On his way south, Wickes encountered an American ship in distress—the *Nancy*. She was carrying hundreds of pounds of precious gunpowder and was being chased down by six British ships. The crew of the *Nancy* grounded her and got the majority of the powder safely on land while Wickes and another ship fended off the British. Tragically, Wickes lost his brother during the engagement, but that didn't stop him from fighting.

A few months after the founding of the United States, Wickes was ordered to transport Benjamin Franklin, the new French liaison, to France, making Wickes the commander of the first official

Continental Navy vessel to operate in European waters. Not satisfied with being merely a passenger transport, Wickes captured two British brigs on the way. After delivering Franklin, he captured a number of British merchant ships in the English Channel and took the ships back to France, where he sold them. Wickes sought cover in French waters, which the French did not appreciate, as they didn't want to antagonize the British. He was repeatedly ordered to leave, but each time he came up with an excuse, such as the need to fix a leaking hull.

Wickes went on to capture many more British merchant ships, including fifteen in a five-day period off the coast of Ireland. After almost a year of capturing enemy prizes in the Atlantic, Wickes set sail for America in October 1777. His ship never made it home. No one but the ship's cook survived, and the ship's wreckage was found on the Newfoundland shore about a month later.

When Wickes's life was cut short, the American cause lost a great hero. Benjamin Franklin called him "a gallant officer, and a very worthy man." As they did for Haraden, the United States Navy named a World War I destroyer after Wickes.

These three privateers—Whipple, Haraden, and Wickes—were employed in a dangerous and profitable profession prior to the war. But during the Revolution, each of them risked everything— not for profit, but to strike a blow for the sake of liberty.

TIMOTHY MURPHY, WILLIAM JASPER, AND FRANCIS MARION

The Musketeers

★ ★ ★

*You equipped me with strength for the battle; you
made those who rise against me sink under me.*

PSALM 18:39, ESV

At the dedication of a monument to an extraordinary Revolutionary War soldier, Franklin Delano Roosevelt said:

> This country has been made by . . . the men
> in the ranks. . . . Our histories should tell us
> more of the men in the ranks, for it was to
> them, more than to the generals, that we were
> indebted for our military victories.

Although Roosevelt was honoring a specific soldier, he was, in a sense, paying tribute to all the unsung heroes of the Revolutionary War.

The man commemorated in the statue was Timothy Murphy. During his day, Murphy's fighting skills quickly made him a legend in the wild back-country. A number of dramatic stories surround his memory—in fact, it's hard to tell where truth ends and myth begins. Those who knew Murphy attested to his incredible marksmanship and extraordinary daring and courage.

Born in 1751 to Irish immigrant parents, Murphy was raised in the frontier, which was constantly under attack by Indian tribes. With a bent for freedom that traced back to early in his life, he wasted no time joining the Revolution. Just about the time the first battles reached him in Northumberland County, Pennsylvania, Murphy and his brother enlisted. His company of fellow riflemen set out for Boston almost immediately, and it wasn't long before he became known as an expert shot. His notable gun earned him the nickname the Double-Barreled Rifleman.

The Pennsylvania riflemen were mostly seasoned hunters. Their guns were far more accurate than the traditional muskets used by the infantry, and they were lethal at twice the range. On top of that, the riflemen had the advantage of being able to navigate the wilderness, making them a stealthy, deadly force. Murphy and his friends fought in the thick of the battle around Boston, maintaining their ground in skirmishes and sneaking potshots at distant soldiers. After the British evacuation, Murphy followed Washington's army to Long Island, Trenton, and Princeton, where he was credited with killing a considerable number of British troops.

In the summer of 1777, Murphy was selected for a team of five hundred riflemen under Daniel Morgan to head north and harass General John Burgoyne's troops. Murphy and his partner, David Elerson, became a famous duo as they captured foraging parties and supplies. Once Murphy recklessly sneaked into the enemy camp at night and abducted a British officer.

At the Battle of Saratoga, Murphy and a couple of other sharpshooters were summoned by Commander Morgan, who pointed out a general who was holding the British line. "I admire and honor him, but it is necessary that he should die; victory for the enemy depends upon him."

Morgan then told Murphy, "Take your station . . . and do your duty." Murphy climbed a nearby tree and, with expert marksmanship, mortally wounded the British general. Then, from an impressive distance, he killed one of the commander's messengers who was relaying vital orders.

Those two shots sent the British into turmoil, allowing the Americans to win the day. The British surrendered the battle shortly thereafter, cementing Murphy's contribution to the war. As one historian put it, "Success at Saratoga was . . . the hinge upon which the Revolution swung. And the bearing point in that hinge was Tim Murphy's rifle bullet."

Sergeant William Jasper, a German immigrant from South Carolina, was another exemplary soldier in the Revolution. He exhibited such gallantry and courage in the fight for liberty that the governor of

South Carolina personally gave him a sword. With a reputation as a trustworthy soldier, Jasper was given considerable leeway by his commander. He was permitted to take men on missions to capture enemy prisoners without his commander even knowing about the expeditions until he returned.

Jasper was also known for his willingness to risk his life for his fellow Patriots. According to one story, a woman named Mrs. Jones came to Jasper and implored him to save her husband. Mr. Jones had sworn allegiance to the king but had changed his mind, so the British were determined to punish him—and likely kill him—for treason. Jasper and his companion, Sergeant Newton, decided to do what they could to save the man.

Mr. Jones was to be transported to Savannah, so Jasper and Newton hid near a spring where they thought the British guards would stop for water. When two of the guards set their rifles beside a tree to get a drink, the two Americans leaped from the bushes, grabbed the muskets, and, almost in unison, shot the two guards. They then clubbed two other guards, seized their loaded muskets, and convinced the remaining stunned British soldiers to surrender.

That is not the end of Jasper's legacy, however. After his company served valiantly at Sullivan's Island, a woman named Mrs. Elliot made and presented the Americans with a flag for their troops. At a later battle in Savannah, two American officers were killed and one wounded when they attempted to plant this flag on enemy territory. As the Americans were about to call retreat, Jasper ran forward to set up the flag himself. Sadly, he was mortally wounded in the act and fell to the ground.

With his dying breath, Jasper was reported to have communicated this to a fellow soldier:

> I have got my furlough. That sword was presented to me by Governor Rutledge . . . give it to my father, and tell him I have worn it in honor. If the old man should weep, tell him his son died in the hope of a better life. Tell Mrs. Elliot that I lost my life supporting the colors which she presented to our regiment. Should you ever see Jones [and] his wife and son, tell them that Jasper is gone, but that the remembrance of that battle, which he fought for them, brought a secret joy into his heart when it was about to stop its motion forever.

Sergeant Jasper passed away moments later, leaving a legacy of heroism and sacrifice for the cause of American liberty.

Many Americans today may know something of Francis Marion through *The Patriot*'s Benjamin Martin (played by Mel Gibson), whose character was loosely based on Marion. Marion was also the inspiration for Leslie Nielsen's fox-tailed hero in Disney's television series *Swamp Fox*. Even so, Marion's true story of perseverance, ingenuity, and valor for the cause of liberty outshines any fictional portrayal and sets an example all modern-day patriots can aspire to.

Born with malformed legs and a short stature, the young Marion set out to overcome his handicaps by embarking on audacious challenges. At fifteen he joined the crew of a ship bound for the West Indies. On his first voyage, the vessel sank after a whale reportedly rammed it. Marion and the other six crew members escaped in a lifeboat, but after a week at sea, he was one of only four rescued alive.

Not content with his near-death experience at sea, Marion joined the South Carolina militia at age twenty-five and participated in the French and Indian War. Marion fought in a vicious campaign against the Cherokee Indians when they dissolved their alliance with Great Britain in the middle of the war. He gained an appreciation for Cherokee guerrilla tactics—notably the way the Cherokee would blend into their surroundings and then ambush their enemies. The lessons he learned in this campaign would come in handy during one of the American Revolution's darkest hours.

Marion joined the Patriot cause early on, believing the American colonies had the right to self-determination. He served in the first South Carolina Provincial Congress in 1775. After the first battles at Lexington and Concord in Massachusetts, the South Carolina Congress voted to form three regiments and commissioned Marion as a captain in the second regiment.

Marion was stationed in Charleston, but when the city's hour of need finally arrived years later, he wasn't there. He had been dining at the home of a fellow officer with several other Patriots when the host initiated a series of toasts to the Patriot cause that made Marion, who did not drink, increasingly uncomfortable. Not wishing to disrupt the festivities, he tried to sneak out, but the doors were locked. He made his way to a second-story window and jumped out of the house, but in so doing, he broke his ankle. As a result, he was away from Charleston recovering when the British took the city in May of 1780.

With Patriot forces in retreat, Marion, still recovering from his ankle injury, determined not to let the British occupy the area uncontested. Drawing on his knowledge of Cherokee guerrilla tactics, he devised a daring plan to disrupt the operations of the British forces, using only about fifty to seventy men. He and his men enjoyed their first major success in August when, using thick foliage for cover, they sneaked up on a British encampment and rescued 150 American prisoners of war. Marion frequently had fewer men than any British force he engaged, but by hiding in the South Carolina swamps, using plant cover to ambush British forces, and keeping his attacks unpredictable, he regularly caused havoc in British operations.

Because Marion's actions not only disrupted British movements but also triggered unrest among locals, who were supposed to be reacclimating to British rule, the British placed a high priority on capturing Marion and his men. One of the officers charged with stopping Marion was Lieutenant

Colonel Banastre Tarleton (who served as the inspiration for *The Patriot*'s dastardly Colonel William Tavington).

Known for his speed, daring, and use of the element of surprise, Tarleton proved to be a worthy adversary for Marion. Serving in the first regiment of dragoon guards, with their green coats and plumed headpieces, Tarleton had numerous successes in New York, New Jersey, Pennsylvania, and then the Carolinas. He and his men routed Patriot militias, instilling panic whenever the American soldiers caught sight of the green-jacketed men. Tarleton proved to be so effective that his commanding officer, General Charles Cornwallis, remarked, "I wish you would get three legions and divide yourself into three parts: We can do no good without you."

But Tarleton was about to meet his match. In November 1780 an escaped prisoner relayed Marion's position to Tarleton, and he immediately set out after Marion and his men, chasing them for seven hours before Marion disappeared into a swamp. This left an exhausted Tarleton to give up, exclaiming with equal parts frustration and condescension, "As for this damned old fox, the devil himself could not catch him." Tarleton's comment spread, and Marion soon earned the nickname Swamp Fox.

As Marion's successes became widely known, so did some stories that were hybrids of truth and fiction. One such story inspired a famous painting, which hangs today in the US Capitol: John Blake White's *General Marion Inviting a British Officer to Share His*

Meal. As the story goes, while Marion's band camped on Snow's Island in South Carolina in early 1781, a British officer came to the camp to discuss a prisoner exchange. Sweet potatoes were roasting on a fire, and after negotiations had concluded, Marion invited the officer to share breakfast with him. That much appears to be true. What may or may not be true is that the resourcefulness of Marion and his men and their dedication to their cause so inspired the British officer that, despite their lack of resources, he immediately decided to join the Patriot cause himself.

The painting conveys several important themes of the Revolution. The British soldier is properly and neatly attired, while Marion's men appear relatively unkempt and less defined in the shadowy swamp setting, evoking a sense of the common man fighting for liberty. Marion is depicted as an effective go-between, being properly attired himself but inviting the British soldier with a sweep of his hand to participate not only in their meal but also in their enterprise.

After the war, Marion retired to the life of a gentleman farmer, but he made several important contributions in his final years. He strongly advocated amnesty for Loyalists, putting his name on

★ ★ ★

"The devil himself could not catch [Marion]."

LIEUTENANT COLONEL BANASTRE TARLETON

the line for reconciliation. He also helped draft the South Carolina Constitution before he passed away in 1795.

Marion will be best remembered, though, for his clever guerrilla tactics that frustrated the British to no end and inspired his fellow countrymen to fight on for liberty. As the once-popular ditty from the *Swamp Fox* show goes:

> *Swamp Fox, Swamp Fox,*
> *Hiding in the glen,*
> *He runs away to fight again.*
> *Got no blankets, got no beds,*
> *Got no roof above our heads;*
> *Got no shelter when it rains,*
> *All we've got is Yankee brains!*

It could be said of each of these soldiers that although they may not have had much in terms of equipment or finances, they had Yankee brains—and Yankee passion. And that was enough to lead them to victory in the fight for freedom.

CHARLES CARROLL
OF CARROLLTON

The Catholic Patriot
Signer of the Declaration of Independence

★ ★ ★

For freedom Christ set us free; so stand firm and
do not submit again to the yoke of slavery.

GALATIANS 5:1, NAB

Today's moviegoers may know Charles Carroll of Carrollton as the dying man in *National Treasure* who knew about a coded map on the back of the Declaration of Independence and made a late-night trip to the White House to tell President Andrew Jackson about the secret treasure buried in New York City. This story is a fabrication, but the truth about the last surviving signer of the Declaration of Independence is even more compelling.

Charles Carroll of Carrollton had much to lose, but also much to gain, from the American Revolution. Though born into a wealthy, influential family in Annapolis, Maryland, Carroll was not permitted to participate in politics—not even to vote—simply because he was Catholic. Ironically, Maryland had been established with the idea of creating a refuge for English Catholics in the colonies in the midst of religious turmoil in Europe. For many years, this colony offered the most religious freedom for Catholics, but they still faced discrimination.

Catholics were a small minority in America at the time of the Revolution, making up roughly 2 percent of the overall population. The anti-Catholic sentiment in the colonies was rooted primarily in the political antagonism between Protestants and Catholics in Europe, particularly when it came to republican forms of government versus monarchies.

This backdrop makes Carroll's story all the more remarkable. At the age of eleven, Carroll was sent to Europe for his education. He spent seventeen years abroad at several universities in France, including the Jesuit College at Saint Omer in Flanders and the college Louis le Grand (named for King Louis XIV) in Paris. There he deepened his religious convictions and gained sharp critical thinking skills that made him an invaluable leader when he returned to Maryland in 1765.

He put those skills to good use, aggressively and publicly opposing the Crown's attempts to tax the colonists without elected representation in the United Kingdom. He also adopted the pseudonym First Citizen in a series of written debates with Daniel Dulany, a scion of one of Maryland's four ruling families. These debates, published by the *Maryland Gazette*, served to sharpen Carroll's thoughts on the proper role of government, even convincing Dulany to agree with him on some of the larger principles. Such powerful arguments coming from Carroll must have surprised many, but it wasn't long before he was given a respected place among those who asserted their God-given rights against a mother country that both intentionally and unintentionally disregarded them.

Carroll's leadership became critical during the Annapolis Tea Party of 1774. This event isn't nearly as well known as the Boston Tea Party the year before, but it reflected an equally fervent opposition to the tea tax demanded by the Crown. Given the combustible situation in the colonies over tea shipments, a British merchant devised a way to sneak a large shipment of tea onto the *Peggy Stewart*, a vessel headed for Annapolis. When the ship arrived, the merchant's business partners in the colonies refused to pay the tax on the tea, but none of the ship's cargo, including fifty-three indentured servants (not slaves), could be off-loaded unless the tax was paid. The ship's co-owner Anthony Stewart knew he could not send the whole cargo, including the indentured servants, back to London, so he agreed to pay the entire tax himself.

There was still a question of what to do with the tea on board the ship. As an elected member of the committee representing his county, Carroll was one of the key negotiators in that discussion. The committee forged an agreement with the ship's owners to off-load the rest of the cargo, burn the tea, and have those responsible for the shipment apologize in the *Gazette* for bringing British tea into Annapolis.

This was not enough for the growing mob of angry taxpayers, so Stewart agreed to destroy his vessel as "punishment" for importing the tea.

Carroll provided a steady and principled but action-oriented presence to the Patriots as they moved toward war. In a supposed exchange with Samuel Chase, another Maryland Patriot (and fellow future signer of the Declaration of Independence), Carroll appeared to acknowledge that war was inevitable. According to the story, Chase asked Carroll what they could resort to if written arguments failed to move the Crown. Carroll's response: "The bayonet. Our arguments will only raise the feeling of the people to that pitch, when open war will be looked to as the arbiter of the dispute."

Even as war commenced, Maryland continued to seek reconciliation with the Crown. Its colonial convention even instructed its delegates to the Continental Congress, as late as January 1776, "to disavow in the most solemn manner, all design in the colonies for independence." Carroll courageously and adamantly opposed his state's position and lobbied successfully for a vote "declaring the United States free and independent states."

Carroll himself was appointed a delegate to the

★ ★ ★

"God grant that this religious liberty may be preserved in these States, to the end of time."

CHARLES CARROLL OF CARROLLTON

Continental Congress on July 4, 1776, and though he arrived in Philadelphia too late to vote for independence himself, he affixed his name to the Declaration of Independence on August 2, signing, "Charles Carroll of Carrollton." He attached this reference to his residence, Carrollton Manor, in almost all of his correspondence so he could distinguish himself from his father, who was also named Charles Carroll. His signature would also leave little doubt to the British which Charles Carroll had signed the Declaration. Carroll was worth two million dollars then, which would translate to about thirty million today. He was arguably the wealthiest man in the colonies, yet he was willing to risk his fortune and his life to stand with the Patriots.

Why was he willing to risk so much? As Carroll put it, "To obtain religious, as well as civil, liberty I entered zealously into the Revolution." All the wealth he had accumulated could not change his second-class standing as a Roman Catholic according to colonial law. As the only Roman Catholic to sign the Declaration, he sent a powerful message to other Catholics in the colonies, encouraging their participation in the Revolution. In addition, having such a wealthy, prominent Catholic sign a document that severed ties to the monarchy did much to improve relations between Protestants and Catholics in America.

Encouraged by the progress he witnessed, Carroll offered up this hope: "God grant that this religious liberty may be preserved in these States, to the end of time, and that all believing in the religion of Christ may practice the leading principle of charity, the basis of every virtue."

In a letter to fellow Continental Congress delegate James McHenry in November 1800, Carroll issued this warning about the young republic he'd helped found: "Without morals a republic cannot subsist any length of time; they therefore who are decrying the Christian religion, whose morality is so sublime & pure, [and] which denounces against the wicked eternal misery, and [which] insured to the good eternal happiness, are undermining the solid foundation of morals, the best security for the duration of free governments."

On July 4, 1826, exactly fifty years to the day after Congress's ratification of the Declaration of Independence, John Adams and Thomas Jefferson both passed away. Their deaths left Charles Carroll of Carrollton as the last remaining and longest-lived signer of the Declaration of Independence. At a time when the average life expectancy was thirty-five, Carroll lived to the remarkable age of ninety-five, passing away on November 14, 1832. His death was a significant moment in the life of this new country—it was, in a sense, the end of an era. The founders had all passed, and the burden of the republic had passed on to a new generation of leaders.

Carroll's final statement, as dictated to a friend, was this: "I have lived to my ninety-sixth year; I have enjoyed continued health, I have been blessed with great wealth, prosperity, and most of the good things which the world can bestow—public approbation, esteem, applause; but what I now look back on with the greatest satisfaction to myself is, that I have practiced the duties of my religion."

With his legacy of championing religious liberty and encouraging Catholic participation in the Revolution, Charles Carroll was a true national treasure.

EMILY GEIGER, ELIZABETH MAXWELL STEELE, PHILLIS WHEATLEY, AND ELIZABETH LEWIS

Patriotic Women

Greater love has no one than this, than to lay down one's life for his friends.
JOHN 15:13, NKJV

Women in the Revolutionary era were perhaps uniquely qualified to grasp the sacrifice required for obtaining liberty. When their husbands went off to fight the British, the women not only had to work to sustain their families by themselves, but they also faced the real possibility that their husbands might never return. Yet many Patriot women were willing to do whatever it took to support the cause. They trusted that God was with them, and they were willing to pay a high price for freedom, even if it meant suffering along the way.

One young South Carolinian woman, believing God had directed her to act, performed a feat so universally admired that it earned her a lasting place on the Palmetto State's official seal. Emily Geiger desperately wanted to aid the Patriot cause, so when the opportunity arose to perform a dangerous mission for General Nathanael Greene, commander of the Patriots' forces in the South, she didn't need to think twice.

General Greene had learned of an opportunity to attack a relatively small British force, but he needed to bring together the various branches of his army, including forces led by General Thomas Sumter. Getting a message to Sumter would be difficult, though, since any messenger would likely have to navigate through British scouts, and no one in Greene's camp was eager to volunteer.

Near Greene's camp lived John Geiger, a farmer of moderate means who was a faithful Patriot but too ill to bear arms. When his daughter, eighteen-year-old Emily, learned of the general's need, she made her way to Greene's camp and asked to speak with him. As the story goes, an attendant showed Geiger into Greene's tent. She curtsied; he bowed.

"I have been told," she said, "that you are in need of a bearer for dispatches to General Sumter."

"I am," he replied.

"Send me," Geiger said.

Astonished, Greene exclaimed, "You? Oh no, child! I could not do that. It is a journey from which brave men hold back."

Geiger was persistent, though, and finally told Greene, "Heaven has sent you a messenger, and you dare not refuse to accept the proffered service when so much is at stake."

Greene relented. "Noble girl! You shall go, and may God speed you and protect you on your journey."

Greene ordered a swift horse for Geiger and gave her the message for Sumter, both orally and in writing. Geiger set off for Sumter's camp, but British scouts soon intercepted her. Not being a particularly good liar, she wasn't able to convince the scouts to fall for her cover story about visiting a relative. The soldiers took her to a nearby home, but being proper British gentlemen, they did not have her searched until they could find a Loyalist woman to do the job. Taking advantage of British chivalry, Geiger tore up the message Greene had given her and ate it piece by piece. According to tradition, the Loyalist matron arrived as she was eating the last piece. Not finding anything on Geiger, the soldiers let her go, and after taking a more circuitous route to avoid detection, she made her way to General Sumter's camp and successfully delivered Greene's message.

Later in the war, General Greene was blessed

"Heaven has sent you a messenger, and you dare not refuse to accept the proffered service when so much is at stake."

EMILY GEIGER

by another unexpected and sacrificial gift from a Patriot woman, an innkeeper named Elizabeth Maxwell Steele. A beleaguered General Greene arrived at her doorstep for breakfast one morning in February 1781. He had been awake most of the night trying to organize and rally local militia after Patriot forces had been ambushed by the British, led by Lieutenant Colonel Banastre Tarleton.

Overhearing Greene describing to his physician the obstacles the Patriots were facing, Steele served Greene his meal, then pulled two bags of money from under her apron. She put them on the table next to Greene's meal, telling him, "Take these, for you will want them, and I can do without them."

Grateful not just for the funds but also for the encouragement for his battered spirits, Greene took a portrait of George III from her wall and wrote on the back, "O, George, hide thy face and mourn," and then faced the portrait against the wall. The portrait and inscription survive to this day and can be found at the Thyatira Presbyterian Church Museum in Salisbury, North Carolina.

Other Patriot women served the cause in more artistic ways—among them a poet named Phillis Wheatley. Born in West Africa in 1753, she was sold into slavery at an early age and transported to Boston in 1761 on the ship *Phillis*, for which she was named. Purchased by prominent merchant John Wheatley, Phillis worked as a domestic servant and companion for matriarch Susanna Wheatley, a devout Christian and a supporter of the well-known minister George Whitefield, a seminal figure in the Great Awakening. Treated more as a family member than as a servant, Wheatley received the education of a young Boston socialite. She studied Latin, geography, history, and religion, and she became familiar with many of the great works of classical and contemporary literature. This strong literary and religious education laid the groundwork for what became her calling: poetry.

Wheatley's masters realized her extraordinary talent and helped her publish several individual poems starting in 1767, along with a book of poetry, *Poems on Various Subjects, Religious and Moral*, which was published in London in 1773. After returning to Boston from London at the end of 1773, the Wheatleys granted Phillis her freedom.

Phillis's poetry reflects a deep sense of gratitude for the Christian faith she had made her own and for God's presence in her life, as well as her fervent belief in the Patriot cause. In a poem entitled "Isaiah LXIII," she writes:

Great God, what light'ning flashes from thine eyes?
What pow'r withstands if thou indignant rise?
Against thy Zion though her foes may rage,
And all their cunning, all their strength engage,
Yet she serenely on thy bosom lies,
Smiles at their arts, and all their force defies.

In one of her most famous poems, "To His Excellency General Washington," Wheatley describes the accolades deservedly poured on George Washington by the forces of liberty:

> *Shall I to Washington their praise recite?*
> *Enough thou know'st them in the fields of fight.*
> *Thee, first in peace and honours—we demand*
> *The grace and glory of thy martial band.*
> *Fam'd for thy valour, for thy virtues more,*
> *Hear every tongue thy guardian aid implore!*

She concludes the poem with this flourish:

> *A crown, a mansion, and a throne that shine,*
> *With gold unfading, WASHINGTON! be thine.*

Washington was so moved by Wheatley's tribute that he wrote her a letter, dated February 28, 1776. His words reveal as much about his own character and humility as they do his appreciation for her writing:

> I thank you most sincerely for your polite notice of me, in the elegant Lines you enclosed; and however undeserving I may be of such encomium and panegyrick, the style and manner exhibit a striking proof of your great poetical Talents. In honour of which, and as a tribute justly due to you, I would have published the Poem, had I not been apprehensive, that, while I only meant to give the World this new instance of your genius,

I might have incurred the imputation of Vanity. This and nothing else, determined me not to give it place in the public Prints.

Wheatley's devotion to Washington and the Patriot cause wasn't limited to her poetry. After marrying grocer John Peters in 1778, she named their son George Washington Peters.

Even today, centuries after her death, Phillis Wheatley is regarded as one of America's finest poets. She used her gift of writing to serve God, her country, and the cause of liberty.

Elizabeth Lewis's story is an example of the ordinary heroism of women who maintained the homestead while suffering the consequences of a war fought on their own soil. Elizabeth's husband, a New York merchant named Francis Lewis, was a signer of the Declaration. While he was away serving his country, the British surrounded the Lewis home in Long Island, New York, by land and by sea, bombarding it from both sides. When a shot struck the floorboard Elizabeth was standing on, her servant begged her to run.

Lewis is said to have responded, "Another shot is not likely to strike the same spot," and she remained where she was.

The British plundered the home and destroyed almost everything before taking Elizabeth Lewis to prison in New York City. Her captors refused to give her a bed or even a change of clothes. An old family servant sent word to the Congress in Philadelphia about how shamefully she was being treated. Thanks to Congress's negotiations, she was released from prison, but the British still did not permit her to leave the city.

Lewis was grateful to her servant for his assistance, and when his health began to fail, she did a favor for him in return. As a Catholic, he longed for a priest to perform last rites, but New York was not a hospitable place for Catholics at the time and no priest was to be found in the city. Elizabeth was able to send a messenger to Philadelphia to procure a priest, who was smuggled through British lines in time to go to her servant's bedside.

The British finally allowed Elizabeth to reunite with her husband in Philadelphia, but she was so frail from her imprisonment that she never fully recovered. Her husband obtained a leave of absence from his duties in the Continental Congress to attend to his wife, who soon passed away.

Emily Geiger, Elizabeth Maxwell Steele, Phillis Wheatley, and Elizabeth Lewis all had different gifts, but they all stand as shining examples of women who contributed to our country's fight for liberty.

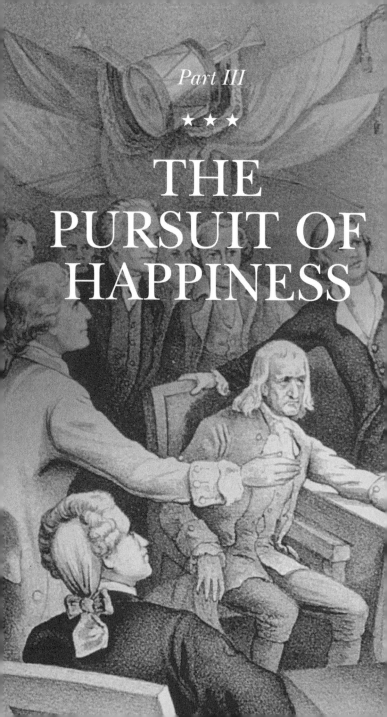

Part III

★ ★ ★

THE PURSUIT OF HAPPINESS

T hroughout the course of my life, I must have read or recited a thousand times the phrase "Life, Liberty and the pursuit of Happiness"—those rights that lie at the heart of American exceptionalism. That said, I have to admit I always felt a little unsatisfied by the words that express the third and final "unalienable" right.

After such consequential and foundational rights as life and liberty, the pursuit of happiness just seemed a bit trite. Did our founders fight and make sacrifices just so Americans would have the right to be happy? Did God give us the right to pursue a good time? Don't get me wrong—happiness is a wonderful emotion and a state to be desired. But is that what our founders really intended to be the pursuit of our country and its people—to be happy?

Let's put it this way: How would you like your tombstone to read, "Here lies [your name]. He/she was happy"?

Count me out!

Isn't life supposed to be more significant than

that? Let's face it—many of life's pleasures are not even good for us, as my waistline constantly reminds me.

But things aren't always what they appear to be. That is certainly the case with the meaning of the phrase "the pursuit of Happiness." It seems that at the time of our founders, happiness had a different implication than mere pleasure, enjoyment, and contentment.

This revelation came to me during a sermon I heard when my wife, Karen, and I attended Cornerstone World Outreach church on a hot August Sunday morning in Sioux City, Iowa, a week before the 2011 Iowa straw poll.

Pastor Cary Gordon exhorted the congregation not to be misled by the word *happiness* in the Declaration of Independence. He related that the common understanding among intellectuals of that era was that happiness was a result of doing what one ought to do according to God's laws. People in Revolutionary times understood that true happiness comes not from pursuing idle pleasures but from doing what God has called us to do. In other words, our founders' call to happiness was really a call to pursue virtue.

One of the great intellectual influences on our founders was the English philosopher John Locke. In his 1690 work "An Essay concerning Human Understanding," he wrote about the pursuit of happiness:

> As, therefore, the highest perfection of intellectual nature lies in a careful and constant pursuit of true and solid happiness; so the care of ourselves, that we mistake not imaginary for real happiness, is the necessary foundation of our liberty. The stronger ties we have to an unalterable pursuit of happiness in general, which is our greatest good, and which, as such, our desires always follow, the more are we free from any necessary determination of our will to any particular action, and from a

necessary compliance with our desire, set upon
any particular, and then appearing preferable,
good, until we have duly examined whether it
has a tendency to, or be inconsistent with, our
real happiness.

The Declaration not only sets forth the reality
of God-given rights but also implicitly states that
with those rights comes the responsibility to exercise them in a way that is consistent with "Nature
and Nature's God"—in other words, to pursue true
happiness.

From its inception, the United States was a
moral enterprise. Our founders, who mentioned
God four times in the Declaration, laid the cornerstone of our country's foundation on the unalienable—that is, nontransferable—God-given rights
of life and liberty to be used to pursue the greatest
good, which to the believers of the day meant God's
will in their lives.

Many have sought to rewrite the history of the

origins of our nation and its founders. The stories that follow in this section are only a small sampling of thousands of Patriots who were motivated by God's call to serve him by sacrificing for a country that was built on his teachings. For them, happiness was synonymous with faith and virtue—principles that were central to America's founding, our struggle for freedom, and our success as a nation and a people.

ELIAS BOUDINOT

God's Patriot

*Oh how I love your law! It is my meditation all the day. Your
commandment makes me wiser than my enemies, for it is ever with me.*

PSALM 119:97-98, ESV

F ew people today recognize the name Elias
Boudinot, much less his contributions to the
founding of this country. But he arguably
worked harder than any other Patriot in preserving
and advancing the moral character of the nation,
especially in his exhaustive rhetorical takedown of
onetime Revolutionary hero Thomas Paine.

The regard for religious liberty was sewn into the
DNA of Elias Boudinot long before his birth. His
Protestant Huguenot great-grandparents, who had
experienced religious persecution under Louis XIV,
fled France and emigrated to New York. Boudinot
was raised with a strong faith as well as a belief that
the pursuit of happiness was intrinsically linked with
the freedom to express that faith publicly.

Boudinot's first love was the church, but since
in his denomination he needed a college degree to

enter the ministry, he settled for his second love: law. In fact, he eventually became the first attorney to be admitted to the US Supreme Court bar. His legal training and his dedication to liberty led him to oppose the abusive legislation the British were imposing on the colonies. Though he initially supported reconciliation with the mother country, he eventually threw in his lot with those advocating independence.

General Washington heard about Boudinot and asked him to serve in the thankless job of commissary general for prisoners—the position charged with ensuring that all British prisoners were guarded and cared for and that all American prisoners were receiving adequate treatment from their British captors. Boudinot initially refused the offer, but Washington, knowing something of Boudinot's character, replied that the American colonies' goal of independence would be unattainable "if men of character and influence would not come forward and join him in his exertions." Boudinot finally accepted, in part "to preserve the Civil Rights of my Fellow Citizens."

Boudinot discharged his duties and then some. Learning of the American prisoners' dire need for provisions and the lack of funds with which to furnish them, he spent almost $45,000 of his own funds to supply these prisoners with necessities. Word spread about Boudinot's dedication, and he gradually stepped into other responsibilities for his country. Between November 1782 and November 1783, he served as president of the Continental Congress, and as such, he was the one who signed a preliminary peace agreement with Great Britain, ratified by Congress on April 15, 1783.

When the new Constitution was ratified, Boudinot served as one of the first four New Jersey members of the House of Representatives. His reliance on God and his gratefulness for God's protection of the young country prompted Boudinot to propose a resolution in his first year as a congressman that established "a day of public thanksgiving and prayer." Boudinot proclaimed that he "could not think of letting the session pass over without offering an opportunity to all the citizens of the United States of joining, with one voice, in returning to Almighty God their sincere thanks for the many blessings he had poured down upon them." President George Washington responded by issuing America's first federal thanksgiving proclamation.

After five more years in Congress, Boudinot became director of the United States Mint. In the midst of his decade-long tenure there, the latent minister in Boudinot made perhaps his greatest contribution to the moral character of the nation with his response to Thomas Paine's *The Age of Reason*.

Patriots had revered Paine for his rousing pamphlet *Common Sense*, which argued that independence was the only viable outcome of the conflict with Great Britain and helped persuade many colonists (including John Laurens) to join the fight. After the war, Paine took aim at religion, arguing for a second revolution against organized religion in his provocative pamphlet *The Age of Reason*. Paine was a professed

Deist, believing in an impersonal God who does not take notice of humankind, answer prayer, or become involved in human affairs.

Near the beginning of his work, Paine left no doubt about his antagonism toward organized religion:

> I do not believe in the creed professed by the Jewish church, by the Roman church, by the Greek church, by the Turkish church, by the Protestant church, nor by any church that I know of. My own mind is my own church.
>
> All national institutions of churches, whether Jewish, Christian, or Turkish, appear to me no other than human inventions, set up to terrify and enslave mankind, and monopolize power and profit.

Paine believed that the Bible "is such a book of lies and contradictions there is no knowing which part to believe, or whether any" and that the only divine revelation he could trust was one he directly experienced himself.

Though Boudinot initially reviewed the pub-

★ ★ ★

"Were you to ask me to recommend the most valuable book in the world, I should fix on the Bible as the most instructive, both to the wise and ignorant."

ELIAS BOUDINOT

lication of this work from a distance, he realized the pseudointellectual arguments Paine was making were influencing younger people who did not know why they believed what they believed. In the absence of any systematic response to Paine's work, Boudinot felt compelled by his inner minister to make a forceful response, overcoming his natural humility for the sake of a battle he considered of utmost importance:

> I am averse to increasing the number of books, unless it be on important occasions, or for useful purposes; but an anxious desire that our country should be preserved from the dreadful evil of becoming enemies to the religion of the Gospel, which I have no doubt, but would be introductive of the dissolution of government and the bonds of civil society; my compliance with the wishes of a few select friends, to make this work public, has been more easily obtained.

Boudinot put his persuasive powers to use in a thorough refutation of Paine's arguments in his 333-page book, aptly titled *The Age of Revelation*. He responded to Paine's critique of the Bible with the following salvo:

> Were you to ask me to recommend the most valuable book in the world, I should fix on the Bible as the most instructive, both to the wise and ignorant. . . . I would make it, in short,

the Alpha and Omega of knowledge; and be assured, that it is for want of understanding the scriptures, both of the Old and New Testament, that so little value is set upon them by the world at large.

In a particularly forceful assault on Paine's claim to reason, Boudinot asserts:

What have reason and philosophy done for near two thousand years, but confirm the glorious doctrine of the cross of Christ, and multiply the followers of the once despised Nazarene. A nation in our day [revolutionary France] has made the attempt to try, what our author calls, reason and philosophy, will do without religion; and let me ask what has been the issue?

Boudinot worked hard in his post-political life to ensure that his beloved country would remain true to the scriptural values of its founders—the only path to true happiness, in Boudinot's opinion. In 1816 he helped found—and served as the first president of—the American Bible Society, whose simple mission was (and still is) to educate people about the Bible and to get this sacred text into the hands of as many individuals as possible.

Boudinot also advocated equal rights for blacks, Jews, and American Indians. He is known for sponsoring a school for American Indians in Connecticut, where one of the students, a Cherokee man named Gallegina Watie, was so impressed with Boudinot that he asked to take Boudinot's name. The younger Boudinot carried on his mentor's passion, working to spread the Bible by translating part of the New Testament into his native tongue. The elder Boudinot also served as president of the American Society for Ameliorating the Condition of the Jews and made personal provision to bring persecuted Jews to America, where unlike in Europe, they could have "asylum of safety."

Throughout his years of public service, Boudinot understood that a country that acknowledged the very real presence of God would be a virtuous, prosperous, happy nation—even a nation capable of minor miracles, such as winning independence from the greatest empire on earth.

CHRISTOPHER LUDWICK

The Gingerbread Man

★ ★ ★

Man shall not live by bread alone; but man lives by every word that proceeds from the mouth of the LORD.

DEUTERONOMY 8:3, NKJV

Today millions of Americans—from infantrymen to oil rig operators to mothers—toil in anonymity, simply doing their jobs with excellence. But as we see from the life of Christopher Ludwick, there is often a great purpose that inspires such commitment. Ludwick knew he wasn't just baking bread; he was doing God's will by providing tangible sustenance in his country's fight for liberty and happiness.

On the most basic level, baking brings together common ingredients, each with a unique function, that work in conjunction to make something greater than the sum of its parts. In a way, the same can be said about an army. Common people with unique functions come together to form a collective unit that is more efficient than each person could be as an individual. And when it comes to war, baking is more than just a metaphor; as Napoleon famously put it, "An army marches on its stomach." Christopher Ludwick, a passionate and committed Patriot, offered a number of his experiences and skills to support the war effort, including his knowledge as a soldier, his experience as an immigrant, and his most famous skill—baking—which led to his position as the chief baker for General Washington's army.

Ludwick was born in 1720 to a baker in Germany. In his early life he went to a free school and learned to bake in the family business. Seeking adventure after his education, he became a soldier in the German emperor's army and fought the Turks for several years. But the fruit doesn't fall far from the tree, so he decided to leave the army to be a baker on board a ship. After a few years he earned enough money to take leave and spend some time at home. On arriving home, he discovered that his father had passed away.

Although Ludwick's father was gone, he had left a lasting legacy for his son. Wherever he went, Ludwick carried with him a silver medallion that had been passed down to him from his father, who had gotten it from his father. On one side of the coin was a representation of John baptizing Jesus, engraved with 1 John 1:7: "The blood of Jesus Christ . . . cleanseth us from all sin." The other side contained these words from Ezekiel 16: "I said unto thee when thou wast in thy blood, Live." With this coin, he was constantly reminded through his travels to take courage in his faith.

After seven years as a common sailor, Ludwick went to London to complete his bakery training. It was there that he acquired a skill he became famous for later in life: making gingerbread. He emigrated to America in 1754 and set up a bakery specializing in gingerbread. A year later he married a young widow, Mrs. Catharine England. Highly respected by his neighbors and associates, he had a reputation for being uncommonly industrious, and he served everyone with integrity and punctuality.

By the time the Revolution was under way, Ludwick had worked hard for many years and had some wealth, including several houses and a farm in addition to the bakery. He risked that wealth by joining the cause of liberty as an elected representative from Pennsylvania in conventions from 1774 to 1776, where he faithfully served and earned the respect of many Founding Fathers. At one point a resolution to buy guns came to the floor, but some legislators objected to paying. Ludwick stood up and said, "Mr. President, I am but a poor gingerbread baker, but put me down for two hundred pounds!" His willingness to sacrifice spurred the legislators to pass the resolution unanimously.

In 1776 he put his military experience to work, volunteering in the army as a Patriot soldier. Ludwick was well liked among the ranks and was often asked to tell stories. He reveled in talking about his home country and how precious America's freedom was to him because of the oppression he had witnessed in Germany.

Ludwick's German heritage was put to practical use as well. Many Germans served as mercenaries for the British army, so he was employed as a translator for captured Germans. This work later inspired him to try his hand at espionage. He successfully infiltrated a British stronghold and talked to the mercenaries there, acting like a deserter. He regaled these fellow Germans with tales of life in America and encouraged them to join the cause. Over the following weeks, hundreds of soldiers deserted the British encampment and joined the American army, many of them ultimately becoming Pennsylvania citizens themselves.

A year after the Declaration of Independence was signed, Christopher Ludwick received a commission from Congress appointing him superintendent of bakers (baker general) for the entire army. This may not have been the most glamorous job, but one of the biggest problems for the colonial army was feeding and equipping the troops. The army ran on bread as the basic staple—one pound of bread a day for each soldier, if it could be provided.

"Mr. President, I am but a poor gingerbread baker, but put me down for two hundred pounds!"

CHRISTOPHER LUDWICK

Yet before Ludwick, no one had really been over-seeing the bread making. The quality of bread was often poor—almost to the point of being inedible. In fact, one loaf was rumored to have stopped a bullet, saving a soldier's life. After Ludwick took over, the quality of bread improved and the army had adequate provisions, even through the hard winter at Valley Forge.

Among his other accomplishments, Ludwick is known for feeding the enemy on one occasion at Washington's request. After Cornwallis surren-dered to General Washington at the Battle of York-town, Washington asked Ludwick to have his men bake more than six thousand pounds of bread for the prisoners.

After his service in the Revolution, Ludwick went back to being a successful businessman in Philadelphia. He was uncommonly generous and even more uncommonly discreet in his philan-thropy. As a result, few specifics are known. How-ever, Dr. Benjamin Rush, a Founding Father and a signer of the Declaration of Independence, wrote a short biography of Ludwick, commenting that "his private charities were like the fires that blazed per-petually upon the Jewish altar."

Ludwick's health was tenuous in the last two years of his life—he was often sick but made the most of his time, devoting himself to reading the Bible, sermons, and religious books. One day in mid-June, he asked his wife to read him a ser-mon (which at the time were commonly printed).

Afterward, he announced that he would be leaving this earth within the week. True to his word, he died a few days later, on June 17, 1801. He was said to be of sound mind up to the end—even as he slipped away, he was praying.

This great American was buried at the Germantown Lutheran Church with an epitaph on his headstone that concludes:

Art thou poor, Venerate his character.
Art thou rich, Imitate his example.

Benjamin Rush wrote that Ludwick's life shows "the influence of a religious education upon moral conduct; of habits, of industry and economy, upon success in all enterprises." Rush said that during the war, Ludwick was well liked, good-humored, and a little eccentric, but above all, he dedicated his life to his country.

Ludwick's legacy lives on to this day. In his will he gave generously to the University of Pennsylvania, several churches, the Pennsylvania Hospital, and the Guardians of the Poor. Out of a sense of gratitude for the free schooling he himself received, he also bequeathed the remainder of his estate, a large sum of money, to go toward starting a fund in Philadelphia to educate poor children from any nation or background. The Christopher Ludwick Foundation still exists and operates near Philadelphia.

Whether he was providing his fellow soldiers

with life-sustaining bread or improving the quality of life for the underprivileged, Ludwick was committed to the gospel of Jesus Christ in word and deed. He will be remembered for the unique talents he contributed to his country—"his zeal in the cause of his country," as George Washington said in a certificate presented to his "honest friend" Christopher Ludwick.

HAYM SALOMON

The Financial Hero

★ ★ ★

A generous man devises generous things, and by generosity he shall stand.

ISAIAH 32:8, NKJV

The crucible of persecution can be a strong motivator. Few Patriots knew this as well as Haym Salomon.

Born in Poland in 1740 to Jewish parents who had fled religious persecution in Portugal, Salomon found himself fighting for the freedom of his native Poland against the Russians. Forced to abandon his country, he made his way to New York City at the end of 1772.

Salomon is best remembered for three distinguishing traits: striking resilience in the face of persecution and injustice, exceptional financial acumen, and an uncanny power of persuasion. All these qualities served him well as he entered the tinderbox of the American Revolution.

Salomon quickly established himself in New York as a successful financial broker. He also developed a natural affinity for the Sons of Liberty, who were protesting British taxation of the American colonists without representation in Parliament, and he soon joined their ranks.

When the British captured New York City in 1776, Salomon was imprisoned for spying. His ability to serve as an interpreter between British soldiers and the German Hessian mercenaries they hired persuaded the British to grant him parole. It wasn't long, however, before he proved too persuasive for his own good. He managed to convince scores of Hessians to join the Patriot cause, thereby earning himself a death sentence.

After bribing his guard with gold coins he had hidden, Salomon fled to Philadelphia, a Patriot capital where he would be relatively safe from recapture. There he reestablished himself as a successful broker and, with his newfound wealth, gave generously to the Patriot cause. He personally aided members of Congress such as James Wilson and James Madison, enabling them to remain in Philadelphia.

Financial hardships gripped the Continental Congress for most of the war, often leading to malnourished and ill-equipped soldiers in the Continental Army. Superintendent of Finance Robert Morris, known as the financier of the Revolution, had loaned large sums of money to keep American soldiers at least a few days away from starvation. Morris knew that might not be enough, so he enlisted Salomon as his assistant.

Salomon's most impressive fund-raising effort

proved to be one of the most consequential feats of the war. When General Washington learned that General Charles Cornwallis was settling his army at Yorktown, Virginia, along the York River, and that the Americans' French allies were planning to send a fleet of ships to the area, Washington realized the tremendous opportunity he had to trap Cornwallis. They could deal a decisive blow to the British, if only he could get his army from New York to southern Virginia. There was just one problem: he needed $20,000 to move his army south, and he didn't have it. Washington wrote to Morris for funds, who replied that he simply could not muster that amount. Washington responded, "Send for Haym Salomon." Salomon put his persuasive powers to the test to help Washington, allowing the Patriots to seize the opportunity and push the war to a successful resolution.

Salomon loved his new country and committed his life to it, in large part because of the opportunities it presented for many people, including those of his Jewish faith. At the time of the Revolution, they comprised just one-tenth of one percent of the population of America. After seeing the persecution his parents had endured for their religion, he proudly served as a trustee of Congregation Mikveh Israel in Philadelphia. Not only did Salomon make the largest personal contribution to the construction of the congregation's main building, but he also played a role in securing contributions from both Robert Morris and Benjamin Franklin.

Salomon guarded America's religious freedoms jealously, and as an upstanding member of his community, he was determined to strike down any threat of religious persecution. When he came to Philadelphia, he was able to enjoy the freedom to practice his faith, but the state of Pennsylvania did not allow Jews and other non-Christians to hold public office. Salomon simply would not stand for this. He and others lobbied successfully for religious freedom that went beyond the mere freedom to worship to the greater freedom to live one's faith openly in word and deed.

After the war, Salomon continued to prove himself invaluable by raising funds to help bail out the fledgling federal government and set it on a path to stability. Eventually, though, the great sacrifices and efforts Salomon had made on behalf of his country began to take their toll. While he'd been imprisoned in New York, his health was severely impaired, and at the end of the war, he contracted tuberculosis. He passed away in 1785 at the age of forty-four. Though he owned $354,000 in Continental securities at his death, inflation had reduced their value to $44,732. Since his estate owed

★ ★ ★

"Haym Salomon was responsible for raising most of the money needed to finance the American Revolution and later to save the new nation from collapse."

1975 COMMEMORATIVE STAMP

$45,292, the man who had been so generous to so many Patriots and had helped keep his country afloat financially died in bankruptcy.

Salomon has received relatively little recognition for his extraordinary efforts toward the American cause. In the 1920s, Congress intended to erect a statue to Salomon, but the financial crash intervened and the project was dropped. He did receive several notable honors during World War II, though. The United States Navy named one of its vessels the *Haym Salomon*. And in 1941 the city of Chicago erected a statue of Washington with Robert Morris and Haym Salomon standing on either side of the general.

A commemorative postage stamp issued for Salomon in 1975 included these words:

> Financial Hero—Businessman and broker Haym Salomon was responsible for raising most of the money needed to finance the American Revolution and later to save the new nation from collapse.

Haym Salomon's critical contribution to the success of the Revolution stood as a great source of pride for the small Jewish population in America. It was also a testament to our founders that individuals from all faith backgrounds had the right to prosper and play key roles in the struggle to create our republic—in other words, they, too, had the opportunity to pursue happiness.

JOHN WITHERSPOON

Humble Hero
Signer of the Declaration of Independence

Choose this day whom you will serve. . . . As for
me and my house, we will serve the LORD.

JOSHUA 24:15, ESV

When it comes to the Declaration of Independence, certain names invariably spring to mind: Jefferson, Franklin, Adams, Hancock.

And then there are the rest of the signers—fifty-two of them, to be exact. And though their names might not be well known, their courage, dedication, and sacrifice were every bit as honorable as that of their more famous counterparts.

In the eighteenth century, with the prevalence of diseases like smallpox, yellow fever, malaria, typhoid, and dysentery, simply getting to the colonies from Europe was a potentially fatal venture, so a certain amount of boldness was required to set foot on the ship in the first place. Some historical accounts indicate that the fatality rate for overseas voyages during the Revolutionary era hovered around 50 percent, meaning burials at sea were common occurrences.

If there was one man who would have been acutely aware of these statistics, it was John Witherspoon. Born in Scotland and trained almost from the cradle to become a minister, he and his wife, Elizabeth, had already buried five of their ten children by 1766, when the call came from the board of trustees at New Jersey College (now known as Princeton University) to fill the role of president.

Having already suffered great personal loss, and knowing the risks associated with crossing the Atlantic, the Witherspoons respectfully declined. But the trustees didn't give up. John Witherspoon was too impressive a candidate to let slip through their fingers.

As a young man, Witherspoon had been sent to one of the best private preparatory schools in Scotland, where he excelled in all areas, especially clarity of thought. At fourteen he enrolled in the University of Edinburgh to continue his studies, and at age sixteen he received a master's degree in theology. After a few years of apprenticeship, he married Elizabeth and settled into a small congregation in the Scottish village of Beith, where he became known for his hard work and devotion to his congregation. During his time there, he became a prolific writer on matters of theology, and his books gained him a reputation as a profound and timely voice in his era.

As a result, the trustees continued trying to convince the famous pastor to pack up his family and move to the colonies. Influential men such as Dr. Benjamin Rush and Richard Stockton (both future signers of the Declaration) begged Witherspoon to reconsider the offer, pointing out the tremendous impact a man of his faith and vision could have on America.

Eventually John and Elizabeth were persuaded, and in 1768 they moved their family to New Jersey. Witherspoon arrived to find the college deeply in debt, the curriculum weak, and the library insufficient at best. He immediately began raising money, both in America and back home in Scotland. A well-read man, he also added three hundred books from his personal collection to the library. Accustomed to the rigorous academic requirements at Edinburgh, Witherspoon increased the entrance requirements as well, establishing the high standard that the prestigious university is known for to this day.

As a result of Witherspoon's tireless dedication, the college quickly grew in both size and quality. With Witherspoon shaping and promoting ideas about the tenets of life and liberty, the school soon became the epicenter for the debate over religious liberty. In fact, Witherspoon's Presbyterian ideals so influenced the colonies that King George III once called the American Revolution "the Presbyterian Rebellion."

Over the course of the next several years, Witherspoon's influence continued to grow, and soon this Scottish preacher was appointed to both the First and Second Continental Congresses. By 1776 Witherspoon had gained a considerable reputation—not only for his tremendous faith, but also for his passionate defense of independence. When the Continental Congress declared a day of national fasting and prayer for the country, Witherspoon was the logical choice to deliver a sermon.

His sermon for the occasion, "The Dominion of Providence over the Passions of Men," became his most famous. In it he warned:

> Unless you are united to him by a lively faith, not the resentment of a haughty monarch, the sword of divine justice hangs over you, and the fullness of divine vengeance shall speedily overtake you.

In other words, hold tight to your faith in God—or be prepared to suffer the consequences.

A short time later, Jefferson, Adams, and others sought Witherspoon's help in editing the Declaration of Independence, which he then signed as one of the official delegates from the state of New Jersey. Witherspoon continued to serve on the Continental Congress until 1782. He hardly missed a meeting, serving on a wide range of committees, including those focused on military and financial matters.

At the conclusion of the war, Witherspoon resigned from Congress and, for the most part, withdrew from public service. But he remained a passionate defender of life, liberty, and faith for the rest of his life. This passion was captured in a Thanksgiving sermon he gave shortly after the war, in which he exhorted the American people:

> To promote true religion is the best and most effectual way of making a virtuous and regular people. Love to God and love to man is the [substance] of religion; when these prevail, civil laws will have little to do. . . . Those who are vested with civil authority ought . . . to promote religion and good morals among all their government.

While Witherspoon may have stood in the shadows of such monumental figures as Thomas Jefferson, Benjamin Franklin, and John Adams, there is no question about his commitment and courage. He was a man with a deep appreciation for the fragility of human life and a man who chose to put not only his own life but also the lives of his wife and children at risk so he could advance the Christian values and ideals he believed in—values that continue to serve as the bedrock of American society today.

★ ★ ★

"Love to God and love to man is the [substance] of religion; when these prevail, civil laws will have little to do."

JOHN WITHERSPOON

RICHARD ALLEN AND LEMUEL HAYNES

The Ministers

And what does the LORD require of you? To act justly and to love mercy and to walk humbly with your God.

MICAH 6:8, NIV

The Revolution was won not only on the battlefields of Bunker Hill, Trenton, and Yorktown but also in the hearts, minds, and souls of the American people.

The Revolutionary era directly followed the Great Awakening, which brought virtue, morality, and faith to the forefront of American civic life in the mid-1700s. It is not an exaggeration to say that the preachers during that time period laid the moral foundation our country was constructed upon.

Many pastors played a significant role in the Revolution. Some, such as Peter Muhlenberg, were dramatic in their involvement. From the pulpit, he read this passage from Ecclesiastes: "To every thing there is a season. . . . A time of war—" and famously tore off his clerical robes to reveal a general's uniform. He rallied his church to join his regiment and fight.

Most pastors, such as Richard Allen and Lemuel Haynes, were less theatrical in their support, but they played just as critical a role in shaping the ideals of the society and promoting virtue and truth. They also had the responsibility of encouraging their flocks as well as providing a personal witness by living out their faith in everyday life.

Richard Allen was born a slave in Philadelphia on February 14, 1760. At a young age, Allen and his family were sold to a planter from Delaware named Sturgis, who, Allen reflected, was a relatively "good master." Tragically, however, Sturgis had to sell Allen's mother and three of his five siblings when Allen was in his teens.

About a year after this heart-wrenching loss, Allen converted to Christianity, finding solace in his newfound faith. Though at first he doubted his salvation, Allen said he "cried to the Lord both night and day" until his "soul was filled" and he knew the Lord had forgiven him for his sins. In no time, he was exhorting his friends and neighbors to turn to the Lord as well. Along with his brother and sister, he found a home in the Methodist Society. (Methodism was a growing new denomination, having reached America just before the Revolution.)

Sturgis allowed Allen and his siblings to attend

church services regularly, despite criticism from his neighbors and friends, who insisted the slaves would become useless if he showed such leniency. Allen and his brother, however, served Sturgis doubly hard as a result. Sturgis was so impressed by their work ethic that he spread the word that "religion made slaves better and not worse."

When Allen wanted to invite the Methodist preacher Freeborn Garrettson to preach to him and his friends on a regular basis, Sturgis agreed. During one sermon, Garrettson warned that come Judgment Day, slaveholders would be "weighed in the balance, and . . . found wanting," and Sturgis is said to have been so convicted by this powerful message that he personally resolved to free every one of his slaves.

Unfortunately, Sturgis couldn't afford to give up his slaves completely. He released Allen and the others to find work so they could earn the money to pay him back for their freedom. Allen eagerly took up the challenge. He worked feverishly, chopping and splitting firewood and driving a salt wagon for the army until finally, after three years of hard work, he had earned roughly $2,000—enough to buy his freedom from Sturgis.

Allen used his newfound freedom to spread the gospel, spending six years traveling the Methodist circuit throughout many of the colonial states. He preached to blacks and whites, men and women of every denomination, traveling on foot until his feet became so blistered and bloodied he could barely walk.

It wasn't long before others started to take notice

of Allen's preaching talents, and in 1786 he was appointed to preach to the racially mixed congregation of St. George's Methodist Church in Philadelphia.

Soon after Allen began serving at St. George's, its black membership grew so large the church could no longer accommodate all its members. Allen suggested they build a separate church specifically for the black members, but the elders rejected his request, opting instead to build a balcony where the black members could sit—separate from the white members.

One day, however, one of the black members, a man by the name of Absalom Jones, decided to sit downstairs in the main congregation among the white members. This act of defiance angered several of the white trustees of the church, and they told Jones to leave. He did—along with the other black members, who were watching the scene unfold from the balcony. Allen saw this mass exodus as a sign from God that it was time for him to build another church for his own flock. So, using his own savings, Allen bought an old blacksmith's shop and turned it into the Bethel African Church.

After seven years, Allen's church had more than tripled in size. It became the first officially recognized black denomination—the African Methodist Episcopal Church—and Allen became the first black deacon to be elected in the Methodist Church.

But perhaps one of Allen's greatest contributions occurred during the yellow fever epidemic of 1793. At the time it was believed that blacks were more resistant to the fever than whites, so at Congress's request, Allen personally organized hundreds of black men and women to visit quarantined houses and care for those afflicted with the sickness. Though the epidemic would ultimately claim upward of four thousand lives, Allen is now remembered for his sacrificial service and bravery both during and after the war. He was willing to give up his own comforts for the sake of following God's call and providing happiness for others.

While Richard Allen gained fame for starting the first black denomination, Lemuel Haynes was the first black pastor ever to lead an all-white congregation. As the illegitimate child of a black man and a woman from a prominent white Connecticut family, Haynes was born with an uncertain future. His mother, anxious to save her own reputation and the family name, abandoned him when he was just five months old.

He was taken in as an indentured servant by a Christian family in Massachusetts who encouraged young Lemuel to get as much education as possible. As he grew up, Haynes spent his days laboring in the fields and his evenings studying every book he

"If you love your children, if you love your country, if you love the God of love, clear your hands from slaves, [burden] not your children or your country with them."

RICHARD ALLEN

could get his hands on—especially the Bible. Determined to become a preacher someday, he even took to writing his own sermons and delivering them around town for practice.

On his twenty-first birthday, when the terms of his indentured servitude expired, Haynes enlisted as a minuteman—a soldier trained to take up arms at a moment's notice. Around this same time, he started writing down his thoughts on liberty and slavery—sometimes in sermon form, sometimes as essays, and sometimes as poetry.

No matter what form his writing took, though, the sentiment was always the same. Haynes was adamant that slavery stood in direct opposition to the basic rights of life, liberty, and the pursuit of happiness that thousands of black soldiers (both slaves and freedmen) were fighting for and dying for—himself included.

In a now-famous treatise called "Liberty Further Extended," Haynes personally called for an end to slavery in America, pointing out the absurdity of slaveholders denying freedom to their slaves at the same time as they were fighting for their own independence:

> We live in a day wherein Liberty & freedom
> is the subject of many millions Concern; and
> the important Struggle hath already caused
> great Effusion of Blood. . . . But . . . we shall
> find that subsisting in the midst of us that
> may with propriety be stilled Oppression, nay,

much greater oppression, than that which Englishmen seem so much to spurn at. I mean an oppression which they, themselves, impose upon others.

He went on to echo the Declaration of Independence in its assertion that "all men are created equal," pointing out that the right to live freely is a right granted to all men by God and is therefore a right that must be upheld:

Every privilege that mankind Enjoy have their Origin from God; and whatever acts are passed in any Earthly Court, which are Derogatory to those Edicts that are passed in the Court of Heaven, the act is void. . . . Shall a man's Color Be the Decisive Criterion whereby to Judge of his natural right? Or Because a man is not of the same color with his Neighbor, shall he Be Deprived of those things that Distinguishes him from the Beasts of the field? God has been pleased to distinguish some men from others, as to natural abilities, But not as to natural right, as they came out of his hands.

Ironically, in spite of all his writings on the God-given equality of the races, Haynes often found himself the victim of racial prejudice—including, of all places, in his own churches.

Because he was fair skinned, he was initially accepted by the predominantly white congregations he served. However, upon discovering his mixed racial heritage, two of his churches asked him to step down from the pulpit—the first after two years, the second after thirty years. Even so, he couldn't be dissuaded from doing what he felt he ought to do—from pursuing true, godly happiness.

Despite his own negative experiences, or perhaps as a result of them, Haynes continued to preach the message of equality, using his favorite book—the Bible—as his compass:

> The Scriptures of divine truth abundantly teach us that all our claims of love to God are vain, if we hate our brother.

Lemuel Haynes died at the age of eighty, his epitaph summing up his life as follows:

> Here lies the dust of a poor hell-deserving sinner, who ventured into eternity trusting wholly on the merits of Christ for salvation.

Throughout their lives, both Allen and Haynes demonstrated similar passions: service to their God and service to their country. They knew that the pursuit of happiness was not merely a matter of thought or action, but also a matter of the soul.

Afterword

I felt moved to write this book for a number of reasons. Having represented the state of Pennsylvania and the Cradle of Liberty— Philadelphia—as a United States senator for twelve years, I wanted to share what I was blessed to be exposed to there: the rich history of the American Revolution. I learned that the Declaration and the Constitution are pieces of living history whose meanings and purposes are diminished and imperfect without historical context.

I wanted to tell the stories of the heroic Patriots, some of whose names have been all but forgotten over the years. They didn't just win our freedom and establish our republic; they were also the pioneers, the template setters for future generations of those who would defend freedom. They were the strong trees from which the fruit of future generations did not fall far.

America is unique in the history of human existence. Prior to the Revolution, monarchs and tyrants ruled the common people. The masses lived to serve the sovereign and were subjected to his will, for ultimately the law was the will of the king. It was not what you knew, but who you knew—and if they were in power. There were no unalienable rights; there was only "might makes right." Rights were not perceived as coming from God; they were deemed as coming from his divine agent on earth—the monarch or the ruler. The more valuable someone was to the ruler, the more rights were allocated to him or her by the king. The converse was also true.

The Patriots featured in this book all knew what it was like to be ruled, and this was a common motivator for each of them to throw off their oppressors. But it was also all they knew, and there hadn't been a successful precedent in history for overthrowing such rulers, much less for establishing democratic self-government. Yet they refused to believe that the status quo would prevail.

Like Americans in the late 1700s, we, too, know that we are living in a consequential time. Today there are fewer kings, but not fewer rulers. Our rulers may not be royalty, but some of them are no less tyrannical, governing the people for the benefit of those who, as George Orwell put it, are "more equal than others."

The threat to liberty is real. It is not coming from a foreign power, although there are serious national security hazards to concern us. There are those in this country who are seeking to return to the historical norm—elites governing the masses. That threat has been with us from our founding, as some individuals in power have sought to exercise it more extensively—allegedly for the benefit of the people.

The Patriots found the courage not to succumb to that tyranny, and so must we. The greatest threat to liberty today is not from the ruling elites; it lies within each one of us when we give in to the temptation to live our lives with conformity, apathy, and complacency. The Patriots in this book could have lived reasonably happy lives if they'd simply submitted to being ruled. In fact, most of their fellow Americans during the Revolution chose that course. It is what every despot ultimately counts on. Despots cannot succeed unless we the people yield to their rule.

Today millions of Americans are questioning who we are as a country and what we will become. Are we still the country that believes in the "golden triangle"—the idea that freedom requires virtue, virtue requires faith, and faith requires freedom? Has our desire for the material things of this world superseded the less tangible rewards of freedom and opportunity?

The level of courage and sacrifice that we are being challenged to muster may pale in comparison with the heroism and sacrifice of the founders described in these pages. That is not for us to judge. It is simply the duty of every generation to meet the challenge of our time in order to maintain our inherent rights—the rights given to us by God himself.

Appendix I

The Declaration of Independence

IN CONGRESS, July 4, 1776.

The unanimous Declaration of the thirteen united States of America,

When in the Course of human events, it becomes necessary for one people to dissolve the political bands which have connected them with another, and to assume among the powers of the earth, the separate and equal station to which the Laws of Nature and of Nature's God entitle them, a decent respect to the opinions of mankind requires that they should declare the causes which impel them to the separation.

We hold these truths to be self-evident, that all men are created equal, that they are endowed by their Creator with certain unalienable Rights, that among these are Life, Liberty and the pursuit of Happiness.—That to secure these rights, Governments are instituted among Men, deriving their just powers from the consent of the governed,—That whenever any Form of Government becomes destructive of these ends, it is the Right of the People to alter or to abolish it, and to institute new Government, laying its foundation on such principles and organizing its powers in such form, as to them shall seem most likely to effect their Safety and Happiness. Prudence, indeed, will dictate that Governments long established should not be changed for light and transient causes; and accordingly all experience hath shewn, that mankind are more disposed to suffer, while evils are sufferable, than to right themselves by abolishing the forms to which they are accustomed. But when a long train of abuses and usurpations, pursuing invariably the same Object evinces a design to reduce them under absolute Despotism, it is their right, it is their duty, to throw off such Government, and to provide new Guards for their future security.—Such has been the patient sufferance of these Colonies; and such is now the necessity which constrains them to alter their former Systems of Government. The history of the present King of Great Britain is a history of repeated injuries and usurpations, all having in direct object the establishment of an absolute Tyranny over these States. To prove this, let Facts be submitted to a candid world.

He has refused his Assent to Laws, the most wholesome and necessary for the public good.

He has forbidden his Governors to pass Laws of immediate and pressing importance, unless suspended in their operation till his Assent should be obtained; and when so suspended, he has utterly neglected to attend to them.

He has refused to pass other Laws for the accommodation of large districts of people, unless those people would relinquish the right of Representation in the Legislature, a right inestimable to them and formidable to tyrants only.

He has called together legislative bodies at places unusual, uncomfortable, and distant from the depository of their public Records, for the sole purpose of fatiguing them into compliance with his measures.

He has dissolved Representative Houses repeatedly, for opposing with manly firmness his invasions on the rights of the people.

He has refused for a long time, after such dissolutions, to cause others to be elected; whereby the Legislative powers, incapable of Annihilation, have returned to the People at large for their exercise; the State remaining in the mean time exposed to all the dangers of invasion from without, and convulsions within.

He has endeavoured to prevent the population of these States; for that purpose obstructing the Laws for Naturalization of Foreigners; refusing to pass others to encourage their migrations hither, and raising the conditions of new Appropriations of Lands.

He has obstructed the Administration of Justice, by refusing his Assent to Laws for establishing Judiciary powers.

He has made Judges dependent on his Will alone, for the tenure of their offices, and the amount and payment of their salaries.

He has erected a multitude of New Offices, and sent hither swarms of Officers to harrass our people, and eat out their substance.

He has kept among us, in times of peace, Standing Armies without the Consent of our legislatures.

He has affected to render the Military independent of and superior to the Civil power.

He has combined with others to subject us to a jurisdiction foreign to our constitution, and unacknowledged by our laws; giving his Assent to their Acts of pretended Legislation:

For Quartering large bodies of armed troops among us:

For protecting them, by a mock Trial, from punishment for any Murders which they should commit on the Inhabitants of these States:

For cutting off our Trade with all parts of the world:

For imposing Taxes on us without our Consent:

For depriving us in many cases, of the benefits of Trial by Jury:

For transporting us beyond Seas to be tried for pretended offences

For abolishing the free System of English Laws in a neighbouring Province, establishing therein an Arbitrary government, and enlarging its Boundaries so as to render it at once an example and fit instrument for introducing the same absolute rule into these Colonies:

For taking away our Charters, abolishing our most valuable Laws, and altering fundamentally the Forms of our Governments:

For suspending our own Legislatures, and declaring themselves invested with power to legislate for us in all cases whatsoever.

He has abdicated Government here, by declaring us out of his Protection and waging War against us.

He has plundered our seas, ravaged our Coasts, burnt our towns, and destroyed the lives of our people.

He is at this time transporting large Armies of foreign Mercenaries to compleat the works of death, desolation and tyranny, already begun with circumstances of Cruelty & perfidy scarcely paralleled in the most barbarous ages, and totally unworthy the Head of a civilized nation.

He has constrained our fellow Citizens taken Captive on the high Seas to bear Arms against their Country, to become the executioners of their friends and Brethren, or to fall themselves by their Hands.

He has excited domestic insurrections amongst us, and has endeavoured to bring on the inhabitants of our frontiers, the merciless Indian Savages, whose known rule of warfare, is an undistinguished destruction of all ages, sexes and conditions.

In every stage of these Oppressions We have Petitioned for Redress in the most humble terms: Our repeated Petitions have been answered only by repeated injury. A Prince whose character is thus marked by every act which may define a Tyrant, is unfit to be the ruler of a free people.

Nor have We been wanting in attentions to our Brittish brethren. We have warned them from time to time of attempts by their legislature to extend an unwarrantable jurisdiction over us. We have reminded them of the circumstances of our emigration and settlement here. We have appealed to their native justice and magnanimity, and we have conjured them by the ties of our common kindred to disavow these usurpations, which, would inevitably interrupt our connections and correspondence. They too have been deaf to the voice of justice and of consanguinity. We must, therefore, acquiesce in the necessity, which denounces our Separation, and hold them, as we hold the rest of mankind, Enemies in War, in Peace Friends.

We, therefore, the Representatives of the united

States of America, in General Congress, Assembled, appealing to the Supreme Judge of the world for the rectitude of our intentions, do, in the Name, and by Authority of the good People of these Colonies, solemnly publish and declare, That these United Colonies are, and of Right ought to be Free and Independent States; that they are Absolved from all Allegiance to the British Crown, and that all political connection between them and the State of Great Britain, is and ought to be totally dissolved; and that as Free and Independent States, they have full Power to levy War, conclude Peace, contract Alliances, establish Commerce, and to do all other Acts and Things which Independent States may of right do. And for the support of this Declaration, with a firm reliance on the protection of divine Providence, we mutually pledge to each other our Lives, our Fortunes and our sacred Honor.

Appendix II

Signers of the Declaration of Independence

COLUMN 1
Button Gwinnett [Georgia]
Lyman Hall [Georgia]
George Walton [Georgia]

COLUMN 2
William Hooper [North Carolina]
Joseph Hewes [North Carolina]
John Penn [North Carolina]
Edward Rutledge [South Carolina]
Thomas Heyward Jr. [South Carolina]
Thomas Lynch Jr. [South Carolina]
Arthur Middleton [South Carolina]

COLUMN 3
John Hancock [Massachusetts]
Samuel Chase [Maryland]
William Paca [Maryland]
Thomas Stone [Maryland]
Charles Carroll of Carrollton [Maryland]
George Wythe [Virginia]
Richard Henry Lee [Virginia]
Thomas Jefferson [Virginia]
Benjamin Harrison [Virginia]
Thomas Nelson Jr. [Virginia]
Francis Lightfoot Lee [Virginia]
Carter Braxton [Virginia]

COLUMN 4
Robert Morris [Pennsylvania]
Benjamin Rush [Pennsylvania]
Benjamin Franklin [Pennsylvania]
John Morton [Pennsylvania]
George Clymer [Pennsylvania]
James Smith [Pennsylvania]
George Taylor [Pennsylvania]
James Wilson [Pennsylvania]
George Ross [Pennsylvania]
Caesar Rodney [Delaware]
George Read [Delaware]
Thomas McKean [Delaware]

COLUMN 5
William Floyd [New York]
Philip Livingston [New York]
Francis Lewis [New York]
Lewis Morris [New York]
Richard Stockton [New Jersey]
John Witherspoon [New Jersey]
Francis Hopkinson [New Jersey]
John Hart [New Jersey]
Abraham Clark [New Jersey]

COLUMN 6
Josiah Bartlett [New Hampshire]
William Whipple [New Hampshire]
Samuel Adams [Massachusetts]
John Adams [Massachusetts]
Robert Treat Paine [Massachusetts]
Elbridge Gerry [Massachusetts]
Stephen Hopkins [Rhode Island]
William Ellery [Rhode Island]
Roger Sherman [Connecticut]
Samuel Huntington [Connecticut]
William Williams [Connecticut]
Oliver Wolcott [Connecticut]
Matthew Thornton [New Hampshire]

Sources

All websites were accessed in July 2012.

LIFE: INTRODUCTION

William Blackstone and Thomas M. Cooley, *Commentaries on the Laws of England* (Chicago: Callaghan and Company, 1884), 129.

PETER FRANCISCO

"About Peter," Society of the Descendants of Peter Francisco, http://www.peterfrancisco.org/aboutpeter.php.

Fred J. Cook, *What Manner of Men: Forgotten Heroes of the American Revolution* (New York: William Morrow, 1959).

JOHN LAURENS

The Army Correspondence of Colonel John Laurens in the Years 1777–8 (New York: Bradford Club, 1867), http://archive.org/stream/armylaurensyear00johnrich#page/16/mode/2up.

Elroy McKendree Avery, *A History of the United States and Its People from Their Earliest Records to the Present Time*, vol. 6 (Cleveland: Burrows Brothers, 1908), 304–5.

John Lauris Blake, *Anecdotes of the American Revolution: Selected from Garden's Anecdotes, Gordon's Letters, New Hampshire Historical Collections, Massachusetts Historical Collections, New York Historical Collections, American Anecdotes, Historical Anecdotes, and Other Works on History and Biography* (Hartford: Sumner & Goodman, 1847), 210.

Paul Finkelman, "Thomas Jefferson and Antislavery: The Myth Goes On," *The Virginia Magazine of History and Biography* 102, no. 2 (April 1994): 193–228.

Worthington Chauncey Ford, ed., *The Writings of George Washington*, vol. 10, 1782–1785, (New York: G. P. Putnam's Sons, 1891), 443.

Alexander Hamilton to John Laurens, letter, August 15, 1872, "Alexander Hamilton: The Man Who Made Modern America," The New-York Historical Society, 2004, http://www.alexanderhamiltonexhibition.org/letters/08_15.html.

"Lieutenant Colonel John Laurens," Yorktown National Battlefield, Virginia, National Park Service, June 16, 2012, http://www.nps.gov/york/historyculture/laurensbio.htm.

"Lt Colonel John Laurens," Valley Forge National Historical Park, Pennsylvania, National Park Service, June 28, 2012, http://www.nps.gov/vafo/historyculture/johnlaurens.htm.

Gregory D. Massey, "Slavery and Liberty in the American Revolution: John Laurens's Black Regiment Proposal," *The Early America Review* 4, no. 3 (winter/spring 2003): http://www.earlyamerica.com/review/2003_winter _spring/slavery_liberty.htm.

Edward McCrady, *The History of South Carolina in the Revolution, 1780–1783* (New York: Macmillan, 1902), 648.

Lorenzo Sabine, *Notes on Duels and Duelling, Alphabetically Arranged, with a Preliminary Historical Essay*, 3rd ed. (Boston: Crosby, Nichols, 1859), 229–30.

A South Carolina Protest against Slavery: Being a Letter from Henry Laurens, Second President of the Continental Congress, to his Son, Colonel John Laurens: Dated Charleston, SC, August 14th, 1776 (New York: G. P. Putnam, 1861), http://www.classicapologetics.com/l/scprotest.pdf.

AUSTIN DABNEY

"Act Emancipating Austin Dabney," Georgia's Virtual Vault, 2006, http://cdm.sos.state.ga.us/cdm4/document.php?CISOROOT= /adhoc&CISOPTR=582&CISOSHOW=579.

"Act for the Relief of Austin Dabney," Georgia's Virtual Vault, 2006, http://cdm.sos.state.ga.us/cdm4/document.php?CISOROOT= /adhoc&CISOPTR=3534&REC=9.

"Austin Dabney's Grave," Georgia Traveler, 2012, http://www.gpb.org /georgia-traveler/season-4/segment/austin-dabneys-grave.

Jim Gigantino, "Austin Dabney (ca. 1765–1830)," The New Georgia Encyclopedia, May 18, 2006, http://www.georgiaencyclopedia.org/nge /Article.jsp?id=h-3298.

Jim Gigantino, "Land Lottery System," The New Georgia Encyclopedia, February 17, 2006, http://www.georgiaencyclopedia.org/nge/Article .jsp?id=h-3299.

George R. Gilmer, *Sketches of Some of the First Settlers of Upper Georgia of the Cherokees, and the Author* (Baltimore, MD: Genealogical Publishing Company, 1965), 165.

"Private Act of Georgia Legislature for the Benefit of Austin Dabney," Southern Campaign American Revolution Pension Statements and Rosters, April 20, 2011, http://revwarapps.org/ga14.pdf.

"Revolution," Flickr, April 5, 2009, http://www.flickr.com/photos /whenlostin/3930905706.

THOMAS NELSON JR.

Emory G. Evans, *Thomas Nelson of Yorktown: Revolutionary Virginian* (Charlottesville, VA: University of Virginia, 1975).

Charles A. Goodrich, *Lives of the Signers to the Declaration of Independence* (Hartford, CT: H. E. Robins, 1849).

Thomas Kindig, "Signers of the Declaration of Independence,"

Independence Hall Association, http://www.ushistory.org/declaration/signers/nelson.htm.

"Nelson House," The Page-Nelson Society of Virginia, April 6, 2006, http://www.carolshouse.com/structures/nelsonhouse.

George Washington to Thomas Nelson Jr., October 27, 1781, George Washington Papers, http://www.loc.gov/teachers/classroommaterials/presentationsandactivities/presentations/timeline/amrev/peace/nelson.html

JAMES ARMISTEAD LAFAYETTE

Ralph Ellison, "James Armistead Lafayette," Benjamin Harrison Society, http://benjamin-harrison-society.org/images/James_Armistead_Lafayette.pdf.

"James Armistead," Virtualology.com, 2000, http://virtualology.com/jamesarmistead/.

"James Armistead Lafayette," Lafayette and Slavery, Skillman and Kirby Libraries, Lafayette College, August 9, 2002, http://academicmuseum.lafayette.edu/special/specialexhibits/slaveryexhibit/onlineexhibit/james.htm.

"Lafayette's Testimonial to James Armistead Lafayette," Lafayette and Slavery, Skillman and Kirby Libraries, Lafayette College, August 9, 2002, http://academicmuseum.lafayette.edu/special/specialexhibits/slaveryexhibit/onlineexhibit/testimonial.htm.

LYDIA DARRAGH

"Lydia Barrington Darragh (1728–1789)," National Women's History Museum, http://www.nwhm.org/education-resources/biography/biographies/lydia-barrington-darragh/.

"Lydia Darragh," Independence Hall Association, 1997–2012, http://www.ushistory.org/march/bio/lydia.htm.

NATHAN HALE

Edward Everett Hale, "Captain Nathan Hale (1755–1776)," The Connecticut Society of the Sons of the American Revolution, 1996–2010, http://www.connecticutsar.org/patriots/hale_nathan.htm.

Mary J. Ortner, "Captain Nathan Hale (1755–1776)," The Connecticut Society of the Sons of the American Revolution, 2001, http://www.connecticutsar.org/patriots/hale_nathan_2.htm.

Linda Tagliaferro, "Nathan Hale Memorial, Halesite, New York," About.com, http://longisland.about.com/od/landmarksattractions/ss/Nathan-Hale-Memorial-Halesite-Ny_4.htm.

NANCY MORGAN HART

John Lauris Blake, *Anecdotes of the American Revolution: Selected from Garden's Anecdotes, Gordon's Letters, New Hampshire Historical Collections, Massachusetts Historical Collections, New York Historical Collections, American Anecdotes, Historical Anecdotes, and Other Works on History and Biography* (Hartford: Sumner & Goodman, 1847), 171–75.

Katherine Brackett, "Nancy Hart's Militia," The New Georgia Encyclopedia, September 17, 2010, http://www.georgiaencyclopedia.org/nge/Article .jsp?id=h-3355.

E. Merton Coulter, "Nancy Hart: Georgia Heroine of the Revolution," *Georgia Historical Quarterly* 39, no. 2 (June 1955): 118–51.

Albrey Diece, "Nancy Morgan Hart (1735–1830)," National Women's History Museum, 2006, http://www.nwhm.org/education-resources /biography/biographies/nancy-morgan-hart.

"Intelligence Techniques," Central Intelligence Agency, March 15, 2007, https://www.cia.gov/library/center-for-the-study-of-intelligence/csi-publications /books-and-monographs/intelligence/intelltech.html.

"Nancy Morgan Hart," Georgia Women of Achievement, 2010, http://www .georgiawomen.org/2010/10/hart-nancy-morgan/.

Clay Ouzts, "Nancy Hart," The New Georgia Encyclopedia, January 29, 2010, http://www.georgiaencyclopedia.org/nge/Article.jsp?id=h-2876.

ABRAHAM WHIPPLE

Sheldon Cohen, *Commodore Abraham Whipple of the Continental Navy: Privateer, Patriot, Pioneer* (Gainesville, FL: University Press of Florida, 2010).

S. P. Hildreth, *Biographical and Historical Memoirs of the Early Pioneer Settlers of Ohio* (Cincinnati, OH: H. W. Derby, 1852), 120–64.

Henrietta Marshall, *This Country of Ours: The Story of the United States* (New York: George H. Doran Company, 1917), 397–405.

Sally D. Wilson, "Who Was Commodore Whipple?," Gaspee Virtual Archives, January 2010, http://www.gaspee.org/AbrahamWhipple.html.

JONATHAN HARADEN

Fred J. Cook, *What Manner of Men: Forgotten Heroes of the American Revolution* (New York: William Morrow, 1959).

Edgar S. Maclay, *A History of American Privateers*, Cambridge Library Collection (Cambridge: Cambridge University Press, 2011), 138–47.

LAMBERT WICKES

William Bell Clark, *Lambert Wickes, Sea Raider and Diplomat: The Story of a Naval Captain of the Revolution* (New Haven, CT: Yale University Press, 1932).

Jack Coggins, *Ships and Seamen of the American Revolution* (Mineola, NY: Dover Publications, 2002), 85–90.

Henrietta Marshall, *This Country of Ours: The Story of the United States* (New York: George H. Doran Company, 1917), 397–405.

"Wickes," Dictionary of American Naval Fighting Ships, Naval Historical Center, http://www.history.navy.mil/danfs/w7/wickes-i.htm.

TIMOTHY MURPHY

Fred J. Cook, *What Manner of Men: Forgotten Heroes of the American Revolution* (New York: William Morrow, 1959).

Lockwood R. Doty, "Timothy Murphy: The Soldier with the 'Larger-than-Life' Reputation," http://www.sullivancampaignlivingstoncounty.com/timothy-murphy.html.

"Revolutionary War Snipers," Top Ten Snipers, Military Channel, http://military.discovery.com/technology/weapons/snipers/snipers-07.html.

Charles Winthrop Sawyer, *Firearms in American History*, vol. 1 (Boston, 1910), 85–90.

"Tim Murphy: Pennsylvania Rifleman," Pennsylvania Jack, http://www.pajack.com/stories/pennsylvania/timmurphy.html.

"Timothy Murphy: Frontier Rifleman," New York State Military Museum, New York State Division of Military and Naval Affairs, March 19, 2008, http://dmna.ny.gov/historic/articles/murphy.html.

WILLIAM JASPER

John Lauris Blake, *Anecdotes of the American Revolution: Selected from Garden's Anecdotes, Gordon's Letters, New Hampshire Historical Collections, Massachusetts Historical Collections, New York Historical Collections, American Anecdotes, Historical Anecdotes, and Other Works on History and Biography* (Hartford: Sumner & Goodman, 1847), 123–25.

FRANCIS MARION

Amy Crawford, "The Swamp Fox," Smithsonian.com, July 1, 2007, http://www.smithsonianmag.com/history-archaeology/biography/fox.html?c=y&page=2.

Robert J. Dilger, "Marion County History," Marion County Economic Development, http://www.polsci.wvu.edu/wv/Marion/marhistory.html.

"Lieutenant Colonel Banastre Tarleton," Cowpens National Battlefield, South Carolina, National Park Service, April 17, 2012, http://www.nps.gov/cowp/historyculture/lieutenant-colonel-banastre-tarleton.htm.

"The Swamp Fox Theme Song," TelevisionTunes.com, 2006–2011, http://www.televisiontunes.com/Swamp_Fox_(The).html.

CHARLES CARROLL OF CARROLLTON

John Adams, "Message from John Adams to the Officers of the First Brigade of the Third Division of the Militia of Massachusetts," October 11, 1798, Beliefnet, http://www.beliefnet.com/resourcelib/docs/115/Message_from_John_Adams_to_the_Officers_of_the_First_Brigade_1.html.

John Buescher, "Are There Instances of Raids Similar to the Boston Tea Party?," TeachingHistory.org, 2010–2012, http://teachinghistory.org/history-content/ask-a-historian/20657.

"Burning of the *Peggy Stewart*," Teaching American History in Maryland, Maryland State Archives, 2001–2005, http://teachingamericanhistorymd .net/000001/000000/000030/html/t30.html.

"Charles Carroll of Carrollton," Biographical Directory of the United States Congress, http://bioguide.congress.gov/scripts/biodisplay.pl?index=c000185.

"Charles Carroll of Carrollton," The Catholic Encyclopedia, New Advent, http://www.newadvent.org/cathen/03379c.htm.

Charles A. Goodrich, *Lives of the Signers to the Declaration of Independence* (Hartford, CT: H. E. Robins, 1849).

Lewis Alexander Leonard, *Life of Charles Carroll of Carrollton* (New York: Moffat, Yard and Company, 1918).

Maryland Gazette Collection, January 9, 1772–September 10, 1779, M 1282, Image 713, Maryland State Archives, October 20, 2006, http://www.msa.md .gov/megafile/msa/speccol/sc4800/sc4872/001282/html/m1282-0713.html.

Maryland Gazette Collection, January 9, 1772–September 10, 1779, M 1282, Image 717, Maryland State Archives, October 20, 2006, http://www.msa.md .gov/megafile/msa/speccol/sc4800/sc4872/001282/html/m1282-0717.html.

Maryland Gazette Collection, January 9, 1772–September 10, 1779, M 1282, Image 718, Maryland State Archives, October 20, 2006, http://www.msa.md .gov/megafile/msa/speccol/sc4800/sc4872/001282/html/m1282-0718.html.

Maryland Gazette Collection, January 9, 1772–September 10, 1779, M 1282, Image 722, Maryland State Archives, October 20, 2006, http://www.msa.md .gov/megafile/msa/speccol/sc4800/sc4872/001282/html/m1282-0722.html.

Maryland Gazette Collection, January 9, 1772–September 10, 1779, M 1282, Image 727, Maryland State Archives, October 20, 2006, http://www.msa.md .gov/megafile/msa/speccol/sc4800/sc4872/001282/html/m1282-0727.html.

Edward C. Papenfuse, "On Being a First Citizen," March 11, 2004, http:// www.msa.md.gov/msa/stagser/s1259/131/html/firstcit04.html.

"Provisional Government of 1774–1776," Maryland State Archives, April 23, 2009, http://www.msa.md.gov/msa/speccol/sc2600/sc2685/genassem/html /gaconvention9.html.

Matthew Spalding, "Faith of Our Fathers," *Crisis*, May 1996, 30–34, http:// www.crisismagazine.com/2011/faith-of-our-fathers.

Bernard C. Steiner, *The Life and Correspondence of James McHenry* (Cleveland: Burrows Brothers, 1907), 475, quoted by Billy Hart, "Charles Carroll of Carrollton—Without morals a republic cannot subsist any length of time," HistoricWords, http://historicwords.com/american-history/charles-carroll-of -carrollton-without-morals-a-republic-cannot-subsist-any-length-of-time.

EMILY GEIGER

Timothy S. Arthur, "A Story of the American Revolution," *The Lost Penny and Other Stories* (Philadelphia: Lippincott & Co., 1862), http://sciway3.net /clark/revolutionarywar/geigeroutline.html.

John Lauris Blake, *Anecdotes of the American Revolution: Selected from Garden's Anecdotes, Gordon's Letters, New Hampshire Historical Collections, Massachusetts Historical Collections, New York Historical Collections, American Anecdotes, Historical Anecdotes, and Other Works on History and Biography* (Hartford: Sumner & Goodman, 1847), 186–88.

Kathleen Maher, "Emily Geiger: Revolutionary Heroine," *Constitution Daily*, April 1, 2011, http://blog.constitutioncenter.org/2011/04/emily-geiger -revolutionary-heroine.

"Who Was Emily Geiger?" National Society of the Daughters of the American Revolution, Emily Geiger Chapter, updated July 11, 2011, http://scdar.org/emily_geiger_dar.htm.

ELIZABETH MAXWELL STEELE

"The Battle of Cowpens," Cowpens National Battlefield, South Carolina, National Park Service, April 16, 2012, http://www.nps.gov/cowp /historyculture/the-battle-of-cowpens.htm.

Tom Belton, "Legendary Women," Women in North Carolina History: Women in War, North Carolina Museum of History, http://ncmuseumofhistory.org /workshops/womenshistory/SESSION3.html.

"Daniel Morgan," Cowpens National Battlefield, South Carolina, National Park Service, April 24, 2012, http://www.nps.gov/cowp/historyculture /daniel-morgan.htm.

"Feb 2, 1781: Nathanael Greene Finds Fortification at Steele's Tavern," History.com, http://www.history.com/this-day-in-history/nathanael-greene-finds -fortification-at-steeles-tavern.

PHILLIS WHEATLEY

Donald R. McClarey, "George Washington and Phillis Wheatley," *The American Catholic*, April 6, 2010, http://the-american-catholic.com/2010 /04/06/george-washington-and-phillis-wheatley.

"Phillis Wheatley," *African Americans and the End of Slavery in Massachusetts*, Massachusetts Historical Society, http://www.masshist.org/endofslavery /?queryID=57.

"Phillis Wheatley: America's First Black Woman Poet," *Early America Review* (Winter 1996), http://www.earlyamerica.com/review/winter96 /wheatley.html.

"Phillis Wheatley, the First African American Published Book of Poetry: September 1, 1773," *America's Story from America's Library*, Library of Congress, http://www.americaslibrary.gov/jb/revolut/jb_revolut_poetslav_1.html.

Phillis Wheatley, collected poetry, http://www.poemhunter.com/phillis -wheatley/poems/page-1/?a=a&l=1&y=.

ELIZABETH LEWIS

"Elizabeth Annesley Lewis," January 6, 2004, http://colonialhall.com/lewis /lewisElizabeth.php.

Harry Clinton Green and Mary Wolcott Green, *The Pioneer Mothers of America: A Record of the More Notable Women of the Early Days of the Country, and Particularly of the Colonial and Revolutionary Periods*, volume 3 (New York: G. P. Putnam's Sons, 1912), 119–26.

THE PURSUIT OF HAPPINESS: INTRODUCTION

John Locke, *An Essay concerning Human Understanding* (London: T. Tegg and Son, 1836), 171.

ELIAS BOUDINOT

Elias Boudinot, *The Age of Revelation, or the Age of Reason Shewn to Be an Age of Infidelity* (Philadelphia: Asbury Dickens, 1801), http://olivercowdery.com /texts/boud1790.htm.

Elias Boudinot, *Journal of Events in the Revolution* (New York: Arno Press, 1968).

The Life, Public Services, Addresses, and Letters of Elias Boudinot, edited by J. J. Boudinot, vols. I, II (New York: Da Capo Press, 1971).

George Adams Boyd, *Elias Boudinot: Patriot and Statesman, 1740-1821* (Princeton, NJ: Princeton University Press, 1952).

Benjamin Franklin to Thomas Paine, date uncertain, http://www.wallbuilders .com/libissuesarticles.asp?id=58.

Laws of the State of New York (Albany, NY: Websters and Skinners, 1820), 241.

Thomas Paine, *The Age of Reason; Being an Investigation of True and Fabulous Theology* (Paris: Barrois, 1794), http://www.deism.com /theageofreason.htm.

Donald W. Whisenhunt, *Elias Boudinot* (Trenton, NJ: The New Jersey Historical Commission, 1975).

CHRISTOPHER LUDWICK

"Christopher Ludwick," General Joseph Martin Chapter TNSSAR, 2004–2009, http://www.josephmartinchapter.org/ludwick.html.

The Christopher Ludwick Foundation, www.ludwickfoundation.org.

Historical Society of Pennsylvania, "Christopher Ludwig, Baker-General in the Army of the United States during the Revolutionary War," *The Pennsylvania Magazine of History and Biography* 16, no. 3 (1892): 343–48.

Benjamin Rush, *An Account of the Life and Character of Christopher Ludwick: Late Citizen of Philadelphia, and Baker-General of the Army of the United States during the Revolutionary War* (Philadelphia: Garden and Thompson, 1831).

Melissa Yates, "Christopher Ludwick (1720–1801): Soldier, Baker, Patriot, Philanthropist," Pennsylvania People, July 1, 2009, http://www1.cbsd.org /curriculum/library/papeople/Pages/1_Ludwick.aspx.

HAYM SALOMON

Bob Blythe, "Haym Salomon," The American Revolution: Lighting Freedom's Flame, National Park Service, December 4, 2008, http://www.nps.gov/revwar/about_the_revolution/haym_salomom.html.

Michael Feldberg, "Haym Salomon: The Rest of the Story," Jewish World Review, 2001, http://www.jewishworldreview.com/jewish/salomon.asp.

Shirley Milgrim, "Mikveh Israel Cemetery," http://www.ushistory.org/mikvehisrael.

Donald N. Moran, "Haym Salomon—The Revolution's Indispensable Financial Genius," Sons of Liberty Chapter, Sons of the American Revolution, October 1999, http://www.revolutionarywararchives.org/salomon.html.

JOHN WITHERSPOON

Raymond Frey, "John Witherspoon: Preacher and Patriot," Hofstra University, http://people.hofstra.edu/alan_j_singer/docket/docket/11.1.17_John_Witherspoon_Preacher_and_Patriot_by_Raymond_Frey.pdf.

Charles A. Goodrich, *Lives of the Signers to the Declaration of Independence* (Hartford, CT: H. E. Robins, 1849).

"John Witherspoon (1722–1794)," ColonialHall.com, December 31, 2003, http://colonialhall.com/witherspoon/witherspoon2.php.

John Witherspoon, "The Dominion of Providence over the Passions of Men (excerpt)," May 17, 1775, TeachingAmericanHistory.org, 2006–2012, http://teachingamericanhistory.org/library/index.asp?document=597.

David Walker Woods, *John Witherspoon* (New York: Fleming H. Revell, 1906).

RICHARD ALLEN

Richard Allen, *The Life, Experience, and Gospel Labours of the Rt. Rev. Richard Allen* (Philadelphia: Martin & Boden, 1833); Documenting the American South, University of North Carolina at Chapel Hill, 2000, http://docsouth.unc.edu/neh/allen/allen.html.

"Bishop Richard Allen—Founder," St. Paul African Methodist Church, http://www.st-paul-ame.org/BRA/index.html.

Steve Klots, *Richard Allen: Religious Leader and Social Activist* (Philadelphia: Chelsea House Publishers, 1991).

"The Reverend Absalom Jones, 1746–1818," Leadership Gallery, The Church Awakens: African-Americans and the Struggle for Justice, http://www.episcopalarchives.org/Afro-Anglican_history/exhibit/leadership/jones.php.

"Richard Allen," *Africans in America*, PBS, http://www.pbs.org/wgbh/aia/part3/3p97.html.

Mark Sidwell, *Free Indeed: Heroes of Black Christian History* (Greenville, SC: BJU Press, 1995).

LEMUEL HAYNES

Thabiti Anyabwile, "Lemuel Haynes: Patriot and Pastor," *Leben*, http://www
.leben.us/index.php/component/content/article/56-volume-3-issue-1/217
-lemuel.hay.

David Barton, "Black Patriots of the American Revolution," Massachusetts
Society, Sons of the American Revolution, May 7, 2011, http://www.massar
.org/features/black-patriots-of-the-american-revolution.

Lemuel Haynes, "Liberty Further Extended," Black Preacher to White
America: The Collected Writings of Lemuel Haynes (Brooklyn: Carlson
Publishing, 1990).

"Lemuel Haynes," *Africans in America*, PBS, http://www.pbs.org/wgbh/aia
/part2/2p29.html.

Carolynn Ranftle, "Reverend Lemuel Haynes," Rutland Historical Society,
http://www.rutlandhistory.com/HayesReverendLemuel.asp.

Mark Sidwell, *Free Indeed: Heroes of Black Christian History* (Greenville, SC:
BJU Press, 1995).

THE DECLARATION OF INDEPENDENCE

"The Charters of Freedom," National Archives, http://www.archives.gov
/exhibits/charters/declaration.html.

SIGNERS OF THE DECLARATION OF INDEPENDENCE

"The Charters of Freedom," National Archives, http://www.archives.gov
/exhibits/charters/declaration.html.

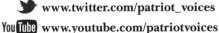